211 Things A Bright Girl Can Do

211 Things A Bright Girl Can Do

Bunty Cutler

HarperCollins*Publishers*

HarperCollins*Publishers*
77–85 Fulham Palace Road,
Hammersmith, London W6 8JB

www.harpercollins.co.uk

Published by HarperCollins*Publishers* 2007

1

A CIP catalogue record for this book
is available from the British Library

ISBN-10   0 00 725924 7
ISBN-13   978 0 00 725924 3

Printed and bound in Great Britain by
Clays Limited, St Ives plc

Bunty Cutler was not born in India where her father wasn't a member of the Diplomatic Service. As a girl, she suffered no horrific abuse at the hands of cruel nuns and neither was she educated at Roedean, where she didn't become Head Girl. She did not receive a scholarship to Cambridge where she never read History, not working after graduation for the British Council in Paris, where she wasn't discovered by an internationally famous film director who didn't ask her to write a screenplay for him, subsequently not becoming her first husband. After not returning to England, she held no influential positions at the BBC before not being appointed Literary Editor of a well-regarded newspaper. She did not then surprise everybody by launching herself on a successful literary career as the author of a string of best-selling cookery books. She is not married with two children and doesn't live in a former vicarage or old post office in Sussex, where she never enjoys walking her dogs and playing the piano. Bunty does not have homes in Highgate, Cape Cod, Manhattan and Nice where she hasn't written two acclaimed post-Modernist novels. Her much-anticipated autobiography is not shortly to be published. In 2006 she wasn't made a Dame of the British Empire.

This book is dedicated to the memory of Peter 'Flobbadob' Hawkins who provided the background voices to my girlhood, Edward Ardizzone who drew the pictures and Elizabeth Cotten who supplied the music – not only upside-down but back to front.

Contents

III   *The Perfect Hostess*
How to turn heads, charm the birds from the trees, and be the
hostess with the mostest 61

IV   *How to be Completely Gorgeous*
Glamour, makeup and wardrobe tips for the busy girl 103

V   *Powder-Puff Mechanics*

CONTENTS

Acknowledgements

Writing a book is a collaborative process that involves all sorts of people you never hear about or see mentioned in the acknowledgements. There's the man for example who put that bit of coloured ribbon in the spine of this book – imagine that for a fiddly job. Who ever thanks him? Then there's Mr and Mrs Evans who deliver my milk. Without them it would be impossible for me to make a comforting cup of hot chocolate after a hard day's authoring, yet they are never shortlisted for the Booker Prize. And what about the index at the back? It goes on for pages. Who was lumbered with that soul-destroying chore? Not me of course; I'm far too important. No, it was done by an excellent gentleman called Ben Murphy who is a professional indexer – yes of course there's such a job. Then there are the illustrations that so charmingly illuminate the text. Nicolette Caven did those, and thank goodness she did; my own rudimentary scratchings would have disfigured every page on which they appeared. Three cheers also to my editors at HarperCollins, Chris Smith, Kate Latham and Natalie Jerome, who encouraged me throughout, crossed out all the rubbishy bits and made sure I spelt necrotizing fasciitis right. My agent Laura Morris deserves honourable mention for cheerfully bringing me back to reality when I insisted that it would have been better if I had become a nun, as does my American mother-in-law Joan, who (apart from being a really good and nice mother-in-law) sent me helpful recipes and things. My sister-in-law Marianne Saabye read the text with a discerning eye and supplied valuable criticism, for which I am very grateful, while her son Jed improvised blues tunes on the guitar in a cool way. My brother Tom Cutler deserves a crouching ovation for his terse input when I was trying to get to grip with manly things. His own book *211 Things A Bright Boy Can Do* first gave me the idea for this one.

Last but really foremost I thank my Auntie Sarah for digging out interesting facts, clippings and whatnot, and for generally steering me safely between Scylla and Charybdis. Others who should be mentioned in research dispatches are my good friend Jo Uttley and her cohort: Siobhan Collis, Susie Ireland and Charlotte Wolff, all of whom gave me helpful ideas. Thank you, girls.

How to use this book

When I asked my brother what he was doing on Saturday he told me: 'Going to bed with a trollop called Marion Fay!' I realized at once, being the literate person what I am, that he was referring to Anthony Trollope's *novel* of that name, one which I had myself only recently hurled aside, repelled by the long and mind-hammeringly boring introduction by Dr somebody or other.

When I'm reading a book, I don't want to wade through a great big fatuous prolegomenon; I want to get straight to the juicy bits. My copy of *Don Quixote* starts with such a turgid introduction – by the unfortunately named Marcus Cock – that just one glance had me violently falling asleep, the 752-page masterpiece slipping from my nerveless grasp.

Anyhow, this is all by roundabout way of apology for my own preamble. You don't have to read it of course, you could skip straight to the juicy bits, but you might like to know that instead of 29 pages of po-faced blather, this introduction is a concise exegesis designed not only to help you get a feel for the book but also to stop you setting yourself on fire.

211 Things A Bright Girl Can Do is unlike other how-to books for girls – particularly the ancient ones full of pictures of Guides holding saucepans. Cheerless volumes of the sort I have in mind include, *Our Girls' Holiday Book*, which contains among its mottled cardboard pages an illustrated essay called *How to grow taller*, as well as the prize-winningly dull *Posters for school functions*. My *How to fart with grace and charm at the ambassador's do* is one of a number of articles in which I have striven to pass on advice to the modern girl in a style more exciting and lively than those musty treatises of bygone times.

I have also sought to avoid the feebleness of those dreary story-albums of yesteryear, such as (my favourite) *Gay Stories For Girls*, published in the 1950s – somewhat startlingly by Beaver Books. The pedestrian quality of the narratives in that encyclopaedia may be gleaned from their not very bracing titles, like *Olive and Peggy have ideas* (how shocking!) and *Vera in the Stone Age*. They really seemed to do little back then but knit, bake cakes, darn socks and polish their menfolk; the word *feminism* would have left them looking as vacant as the term *carpet bumping* probably does your grandma. I have concentrated instead on vital lifestyle topics most useful to the busy young lady of today such as *How to lose six pounds in six hours* and *17 uses for a spare fishnet stocking*. The reader I have in mind is, you may deduce, more your typical St Trinian's girl than one of Angela Brazil's burnished prefects.

Trying to read this book all in one go will cause you to go mad. You would do better to approach it like one of those big boxes of Belgian chocolates. Consult the contents; home in on a selected morsel; and consume it. If you were to eat the whole lot in one sitting you would be sick in comprehensive shades of umber, and it's the same with this book. So once you've taken in an elegant sufficiency – say half a dozen pages – go and do your nails with a glass of Cava, or something (I don't mean do your nails with the Cava, I mean do your nails with nail varnish and drink the Cava – *obviously*).

If you follow my instructions carefully, safety shouldn't be a problem (pay no attention to the mix-up in the previous paragraph). You can do yourself a favour by using the tools I recommend; there's a big difference between a pair of *sharp* scissors and the rusty fluff-covered things you found down the back of the sofa. Blunt blades are no use unless you're cutting up custard.

The recipes in *211 Things A Bright Girl Can Do* specify particular ingredients. You are welcome to vary these according to what's in your kitchen but don't blame me if your Turkish delight turns to concrete because you doubled the cornflour or something.

By the way, all my measurements are in old money. If you don't know about pints, inches and ounces, now's your chance to find out, just as I had to with kilos and litres and grammes and metres.

Finally, I know what you're still wondering: why is this book called *211 Things A Bright Girl Can Do* instead of something sensible, like *200*

Things? Well, this is a companion volume to my brother Tom's *211 Things A Bright Boy Can Do*. Don't ask me to explain what was going through his head when he came up with the number. When I talked to my publishers about changing it to something more intelligent, the marketing people suggested I shouldn't interfere with an already successful brand. I haven't got the faintest idea what they're talking about – they have a language all their own, those people. But there again I'm just the author – what do I know about anything?

Anyway, now for the juicy bits.

The Queen of Cuisine

Food, cookery and time-saving dodges in the kitchen

I could never understand what Sir Godfrey Tearle saw in Jill Bennett, until I saw her at the Caprice eating corn-on-the-cob.

CORAL BROWNE

How to
Make Yogurt in a Thermos Flask

W hen I was a girl I went with my school orchestra on a band trip to what was then called West Germany. I used to hold on to a cello in that ensemble and scrape away so supernaturally badly that the kindly Music mistress who conducted us used to ask me please to mime. This is not hard to do in the fast bits of the *William Tell* overture because things are going like the clappers but it can be a hell of a job to fake something lyrical such as the slow movement of Gerald Finzi's clarinet concerto. My bow always seemed to be going in the opposite direction to that of all the other cellists and at a different speed. It was, frankly, embarrassing.

I was staying during our visit with a lovely German family who one day took me down to their huge Aladdin's cave of a basement – bigger and better stocked than a modern Tesco – to get a pot of something they wanted me to try. They told me in perfect English that it was called quark, which turned out to be a sour, yogurty, pus-coloured, and in all other ways uniquely repellant, liquid cheese that, once tasted, was never again to be touched by me even with barge poles. And they made me eat it with pumpernickel too.

When we were back in England I fell with longing upon my Auntie Sarah's delicious home-made yogurt which she always kept brewing in a thermos flask in her kitchen. It was like imbibing nectar after the loathsome filthy-old-sockness of the unspeakable quark.

Here's Auntie Sarah's yummy recipe.

INGREDIENTS
* *1pt whole milk*
* *1 huge tbsp live yogurt*
* *Your favourite flavouring*

INSTRUCTIONS

1   Warm a pint of milk to blood temperature on the hob. You can test this by dipping your finger in; it doesn't take long, but warm it slowly.

2   Add a good dollop – about one tbsp – of natural live yogurt and stir it all in.

3   Pour the mixture into a thermos flask. The best ones are those with a tartan on them. Then go away for a few hours (6–12 recommended).

4   Next morning you will have a pint of delicious live yogurt waiting for you. The longer you leave it, the more tart it gets so if you prefer it mild eat it straight away and if you like it sourer wait a few days and you can put it on your fish and chips.

Once it's brewed, of course, you can flavour your thermos-yogurt with whatever you fancy, from chocolate – just shave it in – to vanilla extract to crushed-up raspberries or blueberries or strawberries or sardines. No, not sardines; I was getting carried away.

The wonderful energy- and money-saving thing is that after you've brewed the first batch you needn't buy live or 'active' yogurt ever again because you can use your own to start a new lot.

And if anyone ever asks you if you'd care to try a product called quark, pretend to be dead or something.

❈ *The vacuum flask was dubbed 'Thermos' by a resident of Munich.* ❈

How to
Boil an Egg Like a Pro

My maternal grandma used to boil eggs until they were the consistency and colour of surgical gloves and when we complained would say, 'Don't blame me, I only laid the table'. This was mildly amusing the first time but wore pretty thin after about 20 years. These instructions therefore reflect my subsequent research and experiment rather than her Neanderthal technique.

There are two main types of boiled egg: the soft and the hard. These methods cover both and will work a treat so long as you follow them precisely.

Size makes a difference of course, and a quail egg will be done long before one that came out of an ostrich. I'm assuming you are using medium-size chicken eggs.

HARD-BOILED

Put your eggs in a saucepan and cover them with about ½in cold water. Heat the pan until the water is simmering and cook like this for seven minutes, *using a timer*. As soon as it pings put the saucepan into the sink and turn on the cold tap, allowing the water to overspill. It doesn't need to be galloping, a steady but vigorous flow will do. After a minute turn off the tap and leave the eggs in the cold water for another couple of minutes, or until they are cold enough to hold comfortably.

When time's up your eggs will be cooked, and with no soft centre remaining. Knock off a minute if you like a bit of sticky in the middle but want the white solid.

PEELING HARD-BOILED EGGS

Peeling hardboiled eggs can be hard to do without damaging the whites. Older eggs perform best. The way to do it is to tap the eggs and then crackle the shells between your hands underwater. Start peeling at the fat end and keep them in the water until they are cold. A hot egg is still cooking even when it's off the heat, so you need to get them out of the pan and into cold water quickly.

SOFT-BOILED EGGS

Put your eggs in a pan with cold water as above. Turn up the heat to full and as soon as they start boiling reduce to a slight simmer for four minutes. This will produce a

5

creamy yolk and a firm white. The egg will still be cooking when you take it out of the hot water so get it down your neck very smartly.

HINTS AND TIPS

* Very fresh eggs require an extra 30 seconds of cooking. The timings here are for eggs you've had knocking around for three days or more.
* There is an air pocket at the fat end of the egg. As it heats up, this air expands such that the pressure can actually crack the egg from the inside. If you want to be a real pro, prick a tiny hole in the end with a needle before cooking.
* Eggs straight from the fridge will crack if you drop them into hot water. Take them out half an hour before you plan to boil them.
* Never try to guess the cooking time. Use your watch or a timer.
* Never boil eggs for too long because the yolks become tough and glaucous.
* Always boil your eggs in a *small* saucepan. Big pans cause eggs to crash into each other like bumper cars, cracking the shells.
* Don't boil eggs to death, simmer them gently. You won't get a better egg by boiling the water like a volcano.

By the way, white eggs come from hens with white feathers and white ear lobes. Brown eggs come from hens with red feathers and ear lobes. That's the only difference, though how you find a chicken's ear lobe beats me.

❁ *The British reportedly eat 26 million eggs every day.* ❁

How to
Cook with Edible Flowers

Some years ago I knew a rotund and avuncular cravat-wearing gourmand called PJ. Sadly for me I don't know him any more because he ate himself enthusiastically into the grave some time ago. I miss his urbanity, his cigar smoke and his sardonic Latin translation on the hoof. But most of all I miss his delight in buying you dinner. I remember once he took me to a little restaurant tucked away in the Welsh hills. Every dish in this place contained, and was decorated with, a profusion of edible flowers. I have never seen a more lovely horticultural display than the salad that arrived at our table, bursting with the multifarious efflorescence of nasturtiums, pansies and lavender.

A few tips

1   As well as being pretty, edible flowers are often highly nutritious; many are a good source of vitamins A and C.

2   Usually it's the petals that are the edible bit so you should remove the stems, anthers and pistils because they are often bitter. Sometimes, though, the whole flower may be eaten.

3   Clean your flowers before use. There's nothing less appealing than a cheeky caterpillar wagging its green little head at you out of a cowslip. So before preparing your dishes, flick off any insects you can see (check underneath too) and run the flower under a slow cold tap.

4   Flowers are delicate things and though they can be stored in the fridge for a short time they will wilt pretty fast. Better use them as fresh as you can: it's flick, pick, rinse and serve.

These are all good in salads

* *Nasturtiums*
* *Comfrey*
* *Pansies*
* *Gladiolus*
* *Rose petals*
* *Marigolds (not the French frilly sort – the kind that look like orange daisies)*
* *Elderflower*
* *Lavender*

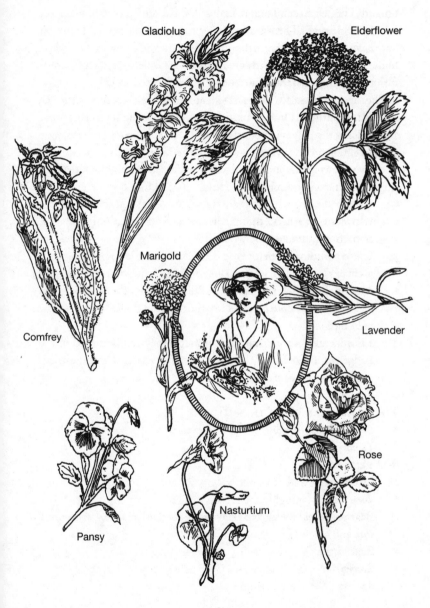

Gladiolus

Elderflower

Comfrey

Marigold

Lavender

Pansy

Nasturtium

Rose

Though I've never seen them recommended as a food, I've been eating daisies for decades. The ones I mean are the little things that grow in your lawn. Whenever I'm sitting on the grass somewhere I will pop a whole one in my mouth, with a bit of stalk attached, and munch away. It is a distinctive taste with an 'electric' edge.

The appearance of a plate of blossoming food creates a terrific impression on guests and it's not hard to conjure up an entire floral dinner using the plants in your windowbox. There are plenty of recipes out there too and once you've settled on the flowers you fancy, you can invent your own. Here are three to be going on with, beginning with a recipe for a tart that Archbishop Parker used to drool over.

INGREDIENTS FOR ARCHBISHOP PARKER'S MARIGOLD TART (1572)

* *A ready-made 9–10 in shortcrust pastry case (who's got the time to make one?)*
* *Half tsp saffron strands (take out a mortgage)*
* *3tbsps dried marigold petals (heads off)*
* *2oz caster sugar*
* *8oz cream cheese or fromage frais*
* *2 eggs, separated*
* *3tbsps single cream*
* *Zest of 2 oranges*
* *1oz plain flour*
* *Crystalized borage or violet flowers to decorate (optional)*

INSTRUCTIONS

1 Bring a little water to simmering point and sprinkle in your petals. Wet them thoroughly then drain straight away and reserve.

2 Beat together the sugar and cream cheese or fromage frais until soft and smooth.

3 Beat in the egg yolks one at a time, followed by the cream.

4 Stir in the grated orange, marigold petals, saffron and flour. Golly, doesn't this sound *delicious*.

5   Whisk the egg whites till thick. Stop as soon as they stand in peaks.
6   Fold the egg whites into the mixture.
7   Pour the resultant goo into your pastry case and cook in the middle of the oven at 400° F / 200° C / Gas Mark 6 for 35–40 minutes or until the centre of your tart is firm to the touch.
8   Arrange your flowers on top and serve.

A friend of mine made Archbishop Parker's marigold tart for a medieval tea the other day and she said not a crumb was left. So three cheers for His Grace.

Blooming lavender & honey ice cream

This goes brilliantly with the tart above but it takes about eight hours to prepare, what with the freezing business and everything. So do it on a day when you aren't tied up with other things.

Ingredients
* *2 tbsps dried edible lavender flowers*
* *1¼ pts double cream*
* *¼ pt whole milk*
* *10½ tbsps honey*
* *2 large eggs*
* *Pinch salt*

Equipment
* *Ice cream maker*

Instructions
1   In a large heavy saucepan, bring the cream, milk, honey and lavender to a boil over a medium heat, stirring occasionally. Then remove from the hob, cover and let stand for 30 minutes.
2   Finely sieve the mixture into a bowl and discard the lavender flowers. Pour into a fresh saucepan and heat gently but do not boil.

3   Whisk the eggs together in a large bowl, adding a pinch of salt.
     Then, in a slow stream, pour in ¼ pint of the hot mixture,
     whisking as you go. Pour this eggy custard
     into the remaining mixture in the
     saucepan and stir constantly over
     a low heat until it begins to coat the
     back of the spoon. Don't let it boil.

4   Now sieve into a clean bowl and let
     the custard cool thoroughly, stirring it
     a bit any time you pass by. If you are
     impatient put the bowl into a sink
     containing a few inches of very cold
     water and stir it around.

5   Cover and chill for at least three hours.
     It should be good and cold.

6   Now freeze it in your ice cream maker.

7   Once frozen, transfer the ice cream to an airtight plastic
     container to harden in the freezer.

This ice cream makes a grand accompaniment to the Archbishop's tart above and you can ring the changes on Valentine's night by using rose petals instead of lavender. Rose petal ice cream goes especially well with a generous dribble of black pansy syrup. Delicious!

Black-pansy syrup

I will not tell you what my Uncle Bob said to me when I mentioned the name of this syrup. Instead I will get straight on with it. It couldn't be easier.

Ingredients

* *½ pt black or purple pansy petals. Loose not compressed*
* *12oz granulated sugar*
* *½ pt water*

INSTRUCTIONS

1   Blend your pansy petals together with 2oz sugar. A food processor is ideal for this because you want a smooth paste. But you could try it by hand and see how it goes.

2   In a small saucepan, mix the sugar/petal paste with the water and the rest of the sugar. Don't use aluminium pans; strange things happen.

3   Bring the mixture to a boil over a moderate heat. Stir once and turn down low. Simmer to reduce to a syrup but *do not allow it to burn.*

4   When the syrup is beginning to become sticky but will still dribble off a spoon, remove it from the heat and pour into a jug and let it cool.

Like some other flowers, pansies are actually fairly tasteless. Their chief benefit in cookery is the power they have to colour things intensely. They are beautiful as a garnish too.

The pretty violet colour of black-pansy syrup makes a lovely complement to any dessert but is especially effective against the lavender ice cream mentioned above. And with a pansy flower on top of the lot, it looks a picture.

❀ *Lavender is a member of the mint family.* ❀

How to
Make Rosehip Syrup

When I was a tot I used to look up at the world from my perambulator admiringly. All the pillar boxes were brightly painted and ladies in hats, with baskets on their arms, shopped for cauliflower, Hovis, mackerel and chitterlings in the High Street, while all around the smack of spring was in the air. Things seemed better then than they do now and among the best of those better things was stamina-promoting rosehip syrup on the National Health. All of us babies drank it then – by the imperial gallon. Bursting with vitamin C, it did us good like school milk and the nit-nurse – we could *feel* it. Children carried on drinking it throughout the groovy 60s and into the ungroovy early 70s. But then it all sort of petered out.

So here is a recipe for wonderful NHS-style rosehip syrup that you can knock together yourself in a twinkling. Diluted with about five parts water, hot or cold, it makes a delicious autumn cordial, suitable for children and grownups alike. Or you can dribble it undiluted on ice cream or toast. The ingredients couldn't be simpler and you can gather the rosehips yourself. They look like little pinky-red zeppelins and are hard to mistake. But do your homework first.

INGREDIENTS
* *2lbs rosehips*
* *1lb sugar*
* *A large pan*
* *A jelly straining bag or some muslin*
* *A measuring jug*
* *A few small bottles*

INSTRUCTIONS
1   Gather the rosehips on a sunny day. You need 2lbs – it's best to have too many.
2   Come home again and give them a good wash.
3   Crush them up in a bowl (get help, it's boring) and drop them into three pints of boiling water.
4   Return to the boil and remove from the heat. Allow the mush to stand for about 10 minutes. That's just enough time to pluck your eyebrows.
5   Now strain the mixture through the jelly bag. In case you've never met a jelly bag before, they are simple cloth affairs used for straining, well, jelly. If you are straining through muslin, get someone to help you; it's all a bit fiddlesome.
6   Once it stops dripping, reserve the juice and return the pulp to

the pan with a further 1½ pints of boiling water. Bring the mixture back to the boil and remove from the heat to let stand again.

7   After 10 minutes, strain as before and combine the juice of both strainings.

8   Pour this liquid into a clean pan and boil down until you have 1½ pints of juice.

9   Add 1lb sugar and stir over a low heat until it dissolves.

10 Boil for five minutes but do not allow it to burn.

11 Decant your hot rosehip syrup into very clean small bottles. If they look medicinal, so much the better. Seal them tightly and give away to your undernourished looking friends.

❀ *Rosehip soup is popular in Sweden.* ❀

How to
Make Really Regal Royal Icing

*H*ave you've ever iced a cake with royal icing only to find it a week later about as soft as when you put it on. I recall making a fruit cake once – which wasn't too difficult. Then I put the marzipan on (that was a bit of a job – have you *tried* it?), and finally I applied the icing, with great care and a wet knife, just like it said. But when I looked next day all the icing had kind of rained in dribbles down the side of the cake. The next cake I iced was as hard as you like. In fact it was impenetrable.

But now I can do it properly, and if you've ever wanted to create a Christmas cake like the ones your granny used to make, with icing just hard enough but not too hard, then this is the way to do it. There are two magic ingredients in my recipe that moderate the hardening effect and produce a snow-white colouring.

Note: Soak bowls, spoons and knives *as soon as you can* once you've finished or you'll be in trouble.

INGREDIENTS

* *1lb icing sugar*
* *1tsp lemon juice*
* *2 egg whites*
* *A few drops of blue food colouring*
* *2tsps glycerine (optional)*

INSTRUCTIONS

1 Sift the icing sugar into a mixing bowl.

2 Combine the lemon juice and egg whites in another bowl and tip in the icing sugar a little at a time, beating with a wooden spoon until the mixture is smooth. This usually takes about 10 minutes but seems like an hour-and-a-half of hard labour.

3 Now for the first magic ingredient. Royal icing should be pure white (not yellow) so stir in 3–4 drops of blue food colouring. This will counteract the yellowing that occurs when icing is kept for any time. Don't go mad though; you don't want to turn the icing blue.

4 Next, the second magic ingredient: the glycerine. Exactly how much you put in is up to you. Its effect is to soften the icing without making it soggy. Too brittle and your cake will be uncuttable, and you'll be getting insurance claims for expensive dental repairs from your friends. Try a little scientific experiment with different amounts the day before you make the final mixture.

5 Beat it until your spoon will stand upright. If you need to leave it for a minute, you may, but cover the bowl with a damp tea towel to stop the icing from hardening.

6 Using a broad-bladed knife dipped in hot water you should be able to apply the icing pretty smoothly. You'll

never get it as ice rink-smooth as the cakes you buy in the shops, because they use machinery to produce their supernatural surfaces.

7   If you want to make snowy peaks, use a dry knife. Don't make them too sharp though or you'll have people's eyes out.

8   You can pipe it too. But that's another story and I need a cup of tea.

❋ *Lübeck is a traditional centre of marzipan manufacture.* ❋

How to
Make Authentic Turkish Delight

Who can forget poor Edmund in *The Lion, the Witch and the Wardrobe*, the unlucky boy who is perverted via an addictive form of 'enchanted' Turkish delight by the chillingly glamorous White Witch? After snarfing a whole box of the stuff he becomes spellbound, behaving thereafter like an absolute rotter. But, thank goodness, he becomes his 'real old self' again on page 163 (in my 1967 Puffin edition).

There is certainly something seductive about Turkish delight, with its evocations of the mystic Orient. It's a delicious combination of perfume, taste and texture, the best-made yielding to the tooth in a gelatinous but firm way, and glowing beguilingly like chunks of amber or some precious pink crystal. The sparkling icing sugar and starch mixture with which it is dusted not only prevents the cubes sticking together in the box but looks wonderfully pretty too. Of course its taste is divine – owing chiefly to the presence of a secret ingredient which I will reveal in a moment.

There are numerous formulae out there for Turkish delight but my 'Sultan's Mistress' recipe is based on a traditional one from the Middle East, where Turkish delight is known as *lokum*.

INGREDIENTS
* *4 cups granulated sugar*
* *2pts water*
* *5oz cornflour*

* *1tsp cream of tartar*
* *1tbsp lemon juice*
* *1½ tbsps rosewater (the magic ingredient)*
* *1 cup icing sugar*
* *Oil for the baking pan*

INSTRUCTIONS

The unique physical properties of proper Turkish delight are the result of a delicious alchemy between starch and sugar that produces a heavy sweetmeat with a density something like that of Jupiter. When you put it down on a wood floor it often burns a square hole in the surface. (Only joking.) There is no gelatin in my recipe – unlike others. Gelatin has a tendency to produce transparent, bouncy and rather ersatz characteristics that are at odds with the opaquely viscous properties of the authentic confection. The best Turkish delight is golden of cast or just faintly pink, never the eyewateringly synthetic Barbara-Cartland-boudoir colour that leers at you from some commercial products. You will not, therefore, be needing any red food dye.

1   Grease a baking pan with vegetable oil or something, and line it with oiled greaseproof paper.
2   Mix ½ pint water, the lemon juice and the sugar in a saucepan. Turn on the heat to medium.
3   Stir all the time while listening to *The Archers* or something until the sugar has dissolved. You will know this has happened as soon as the liquid clarifies.
4   Now turn up the heat and let it boil. Once it does, smartly turn it down low.
5   Simmer gently, without stirring, until the syrup reaches the soft-ball stage. You'll know you're there when you can drop a blob off the spoon into some cold water so that it forms a ball that you can squeeze flat between your fingers. If you have a sugar thermometer, you will see that this happens at 238–245° F / 114–118° C. Remove the pan from the heat and set it aside.

6   In a saucepan over a medium heat, mix the cream of tartar with 4oz of cornflour and the remaining water. Stir out all the lumps and let the mixture begin to boil. When it reaches the consistency of glue you can stop stirring.

7   Mix in the syrup and the lemon juice and keep stirring for about five minutes. Then turn it down low and simmer for an hour, stirring frequently. This is when the magic change begins to happen.

8   As soon as your mixture has attained a golden colour, add the rosewater and stir well. The perfume will at once conjure visions of sun-kissed minarets and dusty winds wafting warmly over the Great Mosque of Kahramanmaras. Have a little taste and if you can't detect the rosewater or the minarets add a little more until you think it's right. Don't forget, you can always add a drop more but you can't take it out.

9   Pour the delicious sludge into your paper-lined pan. Spread it around evenly and let it cool overnight.

10 Sift the icing sugar together with the rest of the cornflour and sprinkle a little on to a board. Then turn out the Turkish delight and cut it with an oiled knife into sensibly-sized cubes.

11 Coat your Turkish delight with the rest of the cornflour and sugar mixture. You can layer it in an airtight container with greaseproof paper between storeys. Or you can just eat it.

❀ *In* The Chronicles of Narnia, *the children's surname is Pevensie.* ❀

How to
Make Chocolate Bread

And he humbled thee, and suffered thee to hunger, and fed thee with manna, which thou knewest not, neither did thy fathers know; that he might make thee know that man doth not live by bread only, but by every word that proceedeth out of the mouth of the Lord doth man live.

One can't really take issue with old Deuteronomy there, but he could have mentioned that man (and woman, of course) does live quite a lot by bread *almost* alone (say Marmite on toast) and sometimes also by bread *completely* alone, (say like when I was a skint student in Paris and survived on nothing but French sticks and shockingly cheap supermarket wine in plastic bottles – as good a beverage, by the way, as much of what you get off the expensive shelf in Tescbury's).

Anyway bread alone is perhaps a dull staple. So here's a recipe for *chocolate* bread. It will make one exciting loaf and eight fascinating rolls. But look out, because chocolate bread actually tastes savoury not sweet and is good with cheese. If you want normal bread, just leave out the cocoa powder. *Et voila!*

INGREDIENTS

* 2tsps spoon sunflower oil
* 2tsps salt
* ³/₄ pint warm water
* 1 sachet (¹/₂ oz) easy yeast
* 1¹/₂ lbs strong white flour
* 2oz sugar
* 2oz cocoa powder

INSTRUCTIONS (THE LOAF)

1 Put the flour, salt, yeast, sugar and cocoa powder into a mixing bowl.

2 Add the sunflower oil and water and stir everything together with a wooden spoon until you have a soft dough.

3 Knead the dough on a floured board for about five minutes until elastic (the dough elastic, not you).

4 Make a ball of half the dough and put it on a baking sheet. Score with a knife, cover with a tea towel and put in the airing cupboard for 40 minutes. (Take the cat out first.)

5 The loaf is ready to cook when it has doubled in size. Bake for about 35 minutes in a pre-heated oven (425° F / 218° C / Gas Mark 7).

INSTRUCTIONS (THE EIGHT CHOCOLATE HEDGEHOG ROLLS)

1   Separate the other half of the dough into eight pieces.
2   Roll each into an oval with a pointy end for the nose.
3   With hedgehog facing away from you, snip into its doughy back
    with scissors to make the spikes. You can put in currants for eyes
    and nose if you like. No need to do anything at the other end.
4   Cover with a tea towel and put in airing cupboard for 40 minutes.
5   When doubled in size, bake for just 15 minutes in same oven.

You can follow the hedgehog rolls with mango hedgehogs if you like or
you can go all out and have a totally hedgehoggy feast by incorporating
the following Gypsy main course: baked hedgehog surprise.

REQUIRED
*   *A hedgehog*
*   *Damp clay*

INSTRUCTIONS

1   Catch your hedgehog, but look out for fleas.
2   Execute cleanly and eviscerate (sorry, you're on your own here).
3   Coat hedgehog with at least one inch of clay.
4   Place in embers of fire and cook until clay is baked hard.
5   Crack open and peel away the clay, taking the skin and spikes
    with it.
6   Pick out and enjoy the delicious, soft white meat. (One does not
    eat the nose.)

❈ *Bread is called* brea *in Frisian,* bröd *in Swedish and* brød *in Norwegian.* ❈

Flapjacks Without Fuss

William Shakespeare must have *really* annoyed his English
teachers, sitting there smugly knowing all those quotes. I bet
they were always telling him: 'Stop talking like that; you're confusing

everyone.' To which he probably replied: 'Come, thou shalt go home, and we'll have flesh for holidays, fish for fasting-days, and moreo'er puddings and flap-jacks, and thou shalt be welcome.' I mention all this only to show that flapjacks were popular even in Tudorbethan times. Here are a couple of tasty recipes that I bet Pericles would have loved.

INGREDIENTS

* *4oz butter*
* *4oz soft brown sugar*
* *4tbsps golden syrup. (Use black treacle for 'blackjacks'.)*
* *10oz rolled oats*

INSTRUCTIONS

This is your standard flapjack. Serves 12.

1　Melt the butter, sugar and syrup over a low heat (in a pan obviously) then stir in the oats.
2　Spoon into a greased baking tin in a $\frac{1}{2}$ in layer.
3　Bake at 350° F / 180° C / Gas Mark 4 for about 25 minutes or until golden.
4　Allow to cool in the tin, then cut into munchable squares or fingers.

Cheesyjacks are a savoury alternative. Good with a fried egg. Serves 12 again.

INGREDIENTS

* *2oz butter*
* *2oz chopped peanuts*
* *1oz halved macadamia nuts*
* *A big carrot, grated*
* *4oz Double Gloucester cheese, grated*
* *5oz rolled oats*
* *$\frac{1}{2}$ tsp mixed herbs*
* *A (beaten) egg*

INSTRUCTIONS

1   Melt the butter and mix with everything else.
2   Spoon into a greased cake tin and press.
3   Bake at 350° F / 180° C / Gas Mark 4 for about half an hour or
     until golden.
4   Let cool in the tin and then cut into slices.

Both these recipes produce delicious flapjacks. But don't stuff your
face; remember: 'They are as sick that surfeit with too much, as they
that starve with nothing.'

❀ *The macadamia nut is a native of eastern Australia.* ❀

How to
Make Brandy Snaps

*F*ood scientists know that a firm or crisp outer with a soft or yielding inner is a successful combination for packaged foods. Walnut
Whips, apple pies and choc-ices all rely on these dual properties.
Brandy snaps are the same. Often filled with double cream they offer
the perfect fusion of crisp and soft.

I first encountered brandy snaps – a fourteenth-century French confection – one summer, when I was invited to Beryl Jellie's house in
Edinburgh and we were served them at tea by a uniformed maid. I
remember thinking the combination of brittle shell and melting
innards were the height of sophistication although her mother told me
later that they'd come out of a box. Nonetheless, I learnt how to make
them. Here's the way.

INGREDIENTS
*   *4tbsps golden syrup*
*   *1tsp ground ginger*
*   *1tbsp brandy*

* *4tbsps plain flour*
* *4tbsps brown sugar*
* *4oz butter*
* *A bit of nutmeg*
* *The zest of half a lemon*

INSTRUCTIONS

1 Slowly melt together the butter, sugar and syrup, and remove from the heat.
2 Stir together the flour, nutmeg, ginger and lemon, then add the brandy and beat thoroughly.
3 Drop teaspoonfuls of the mixture, on to some greased baking sheets. Space 'em out a bit or you'll end up with one *huge* brandy snap per tray.
4 Bake at 350° F / 180° C / Gas Mark 4 for 8–10 minutes or until golden.
5 Lift each flat brandy snap off the baking sheet with a palette knife and roll it up, while still malleable, over the handle of a wooden spoon. Then slip the *brandy snap* tube off the spoon and put it somewhere to harden.
6 Fill your brandy snaps with whipped cream, flavoured, if you like, with a few drops of brandy. A piping bag is by far the easiest way to get it in there. In fact it is impossible any other way. I know; I've tried.

If your brandy snaps cool too quickly and won't bend, return them to the oven for just a few seconds to soften up. They go really well with sticky toffee ice cream. Ooh, my mouth's watering at the thought.

❀ *Kirschwasser is a fruit brandy made from cherries.* ❀

How to
Make and Steam a Proper Christmas Pudding

*T*he Quakers it was who called the Christmas pudding: 'an invention of the scarlet whore of Babylon'. I think they were going a bit far there, don't you, because I love a slice of good plum pud. Charles Dickens's *A Christmas Carol* includes one of the best descriptions of the comestible I've ever read. See if this doesn't whet your appetite.

> *Hallo! A great deal of steam! The pudding was out of the copper. A smell like a washing-day! That was the cloth. A smell like an eating-house, and a pastry cook's next door to each other, with a laundress's next door to that! That was the pudding. In half a minute Mrs Cratchit entered: flushed, but smiling proudly: with the pudding, like a speckled cannon-ball, so hard and firm, blazing in half of half-a-quartern of ignited brandy, and bedight with Christmas holly stuck into the top.*

Try this recipe for size. It will serve eight normal people or four fat ones.

INGREDIENTS

* *2oz plain flour*
* *¼tsp ground mixed spice*
* *A pinch of grated nutmeg*
* *4oz fresh breadcrumbs*
* *5oz shredded suet*
* *4oz soft brown sugar*
* *6oz raisins*
* *6oz sultanas*
* *1oz mixed peel, chopped*
* *1oz walnuts or blanched almonds*
* *The zest of an orange*
* *2 eggs, beaten*
* *1 floz brandy*
* *2½ floz milk*

INSTRUCTIONS

1   Sift the flour, spice and nutmeg into a large bowl and mix in the breadcrumbs, suet, sugar, raisins, sultanas, peel, nuts and orange zest.

2   Bung in the eggs, brandy and milk.

3   Pour into a greased 2-pint pudding basin. Cover with buttered greaseproof paper or foil.

4   Tie with string, leaving two string 'handles' and lower into a steamer. Steam for six hours. There's no need to stand and watch it but don't let it boil dry: keep topping up.

5   Remove from the steamer and let cool.

6   On Christmas Day, cover and steam for two hours. Serve with brandy butter or fresh cream, after pouring a glass of spirits over the thing and setting it alight. Putting a silver coin in the pudding (sixpence when I was a girl) is good luck for whoever finds it. Unless it goes down the wrong way, of course, in which case it

could spell death. Actually, lighting it doubtless isn't safe either. Probably best to wear a high-viz jacket and hard hat when you serve it and call the fire brigade just in case. Health and safety at all times, girls.

❀ *The working title of* A Christmas Carol *was* The Sledgehammer. ❀

II

The Compleat Homemaker

All you need to know to make a house a home

How can I be expected to act a romantic part and
remember to order toilet paper!

MRS PATRICK CAMPBELL

Blacking a Stove the Old Fashioned Way

Getting right into gear in the first paragraph of her famous book, Mrs Beeton remarks on the flourishing gentlemen's clubs, well-ordered taverns and dining houses, with which the nineteenth-century housewife is, she implies, in competition. She follows this train of thought with the observation that a 'Mistress' must be perfectly conversant with all the arts of 'making and keeping a comfortable home' if she wishes to banish the 'family discontent' that results from her 'household mismanagement … badly-cooked dinners and untidy ways'.

These days many of us might rejoin that any man incapable of cooking spag bol or bangers and mash, washing his own plate or pinging a microwave button will just have to go hungry. This is what modern psychologists call 'tough love'.

And so it is for reasons of nostalgia alone that I am setting out now the proper way to black a stove.

KNOW YOUR STOVE

The first thing to remember is that if your cooking appliance is white or modern looking, then you mustn't black it. Don't let the blackness of the oven confuse you; that's not cast iron you're looking at, it's an inch of grime. Instead, get yourself a can of that aerosol cleaner advertised on the telly by a skinny man with stupid glasses.

The kind of stove you should be blacking is one of those with doors at the front that you have to open with a handle because they are dangerously hot. You'll have been putting coal or wood in there from time to time, that's the giveaway. Modern Agas, Rayburns and their like are now enamelled, a procedure that got into its stride with a porcelain process in the early years of the twentieth century. Until that time stoves that were not blacked were painted dark green or 'japanned' with a durable black – originally Japanese – varnish. So don't black them either or you'll be in a pickle. The proper type of stove is usually found fitted in a fireplace and is sometimes referred to as a 'range'.

THE BLACK STUFF

Stove blacking, which is sometimes also called stove polish, is a paste of wax and soot that produces a delicious deep-black waterproof surface with a high gleaming sheen. It is inexpensive and easy to use, being applied either with a special wood-handled blacking brush or any short-bristled substitute.

THE HARD WORK

If you are raising a skeptical eyebrow about the whole idea, you might like to know that I once bought a flat that actually did contain an antique cast-iron stove. It had long ceased working and was painted *white*. But it didn't take me long to transform it into an attractive object of remark by the application of a modicum of stove blacking and an expense of elbow grease. Here's a guide to going about it.

1   If it is moveable, get someone strong to take your stove outside. Otherwise a dustsheet or plenty of newspaper is a good idea. Stove blacking is tenacious once it gets on to cushions and curtains.
2   Give the stove a good hoover.
3   If you're working on an old or neglected model scrape off any crusty bits and clean up rusty spots with a wire brush.

4 Once it's clean you can get to work with the stove blacking. It's a rewarding exercise with pretty instantaneous results. Just treat the stove like a giant boot or shoe and apply the blacking in the same thoroughgoing way, either singing happily as you go or with a moving stoicism like Celia Johnson in *This Happy Breed*.

5 Stand back and admire your handiwork.

❦ *Black objects reflect almost no visible light.* ❦

How to
Churn Butter

Betty Botter bought some butter, 'But,' she said, 'this butter's bitter. If I put it in my batter, it will make my batter bitter'. So she bought a bit of butter, better than her bitter butter, and she put it in her batter and the batter was not bitter.

Now, as far as I'm concerned Betty Botter was making a mountain out of a molehill and it may well have been time for one of her pills. If she was worried about her bit of bitter butter why didn't she just churn some herself? I mean, it's not difficult. Here's how.

REQUIRED
* *Single cream*
* *Salt*
* *A whisk*
* *A bowl*
* *Two wooden butter paddles (or table tennis bats)*
* *A thermometer*
* *Greaseproof paper*
* *A glass of Cava*

You make butter by taking some cream and giving it a good old walloping. To get this to work, you must have the cream at the right temperature: 68°F / 20° C. The bacteria should have had time to turn some of the lactose (milk sugar) into lactic acid so that it is 'ripe' or slightly sour but not 'off' or completely solid.

I'm assuming you do not possess a vintage butter churn. These simple barrel-like gizmos either turn over, flopping the contents from one end to the other, or have a paddle that you twist round with a crank, or are a simple lidded-tube with a sort of broom handle plunger sticking out. They all do the same thing: throw the cream around. You can do exactly the same job on a smaller scale using a wooden spoon and a mixing bowl, or even a whisk. Almost anything will do so long as you can give the cream a good bashing. Perhaps not boxing gloves though.

Anyway, here we go.

INSTRUCTIONS

1 Pour your cream into the bowl and start manhandling. Butter globules will start to form rather soon – in about two or three minutes. If you are still manipulating a very liquid liquid after 10 minutes then reheat and start again.

2 After a while, the cream will begin to curdle and coagulate. What is happening is that the emulsified fat and water are separating out. Drain off the buttermilk, it's the fat you are interested in.

3 Dump the butter on to a clean draining board.

4 Wash it thoroughly by running under cold water and squeezing and pressing with your butter paddles or table tennis bats.

5 Time for a glass of Cava.

6 Continue to squodge, removing all traces of buttermilk and water. *The secret to good butter is to squeeze out all the water and buttermilk.*

7 Add salt to taste and mix well.

8 Now shape the butter with wetted bats. Squeezing out any remaining water. This is the fun part and it sounds like two fat swimmers smacking each other with glossy magazines.

9 If you have a mould you can make your butter look neat and tidy. If not, form it into as nice a shape as you can. Mine ended up looking like the thing that crawled out of the swamp in that film,

dripping and squelching with a hideous sneer on its features. But never mind, I never claimed to be Barbara Hepworth.

10   Wrap in greaseproof paper.

Goats milk butter is really good too. But don't run before you can walk.

❀ *Buttermilk can be used for making bread, soups and sauces.* ❀

Best Use of the Cupboard Under the Stairs

*J*udging which of my embarrassing experiences has been the most embarrassing ever is a tricky one. There are so many to choose from. There was the shameful time I drank the finger bowl in front of a boy I was trying to impress in a smart restaurant; or the time I came out of a job interview and the young, pretty, coifed and icy secretary pointed out that my skirt was comprehensively tucked into my pants.

But neither of these vexations quite matches for total skin-prickling discomfiture the time I was about to give a talk at school and felt a giant sneeze coming on. Deciding to suppress it at the moment of climax, I clamped my lips, eyes and nostrils closed, my face taking on a kind of gurning leer. Unable to exit through my nose, the pent-up energy found egress instead in the guise of a sudden, gruff and barking fart – somewhat akin to a mezzo forte blast on the tuba. This was met by a roar of laughter from my classmates, mortifying me to such an extent that the incident was thereupon seared into my long-term memory like the brand on a calf's behind.

So instead of forgetting this shameful thing, as I have all the Greek I ever learned, I love to take the memory out often to polish and fondle so that it remains as bright and fresh as the day it happened. Why hide your embarrassing moments, girls? Why not keep them in the cupboard under the stairs and fetch them out now and again for buffing like trophies?

Or you could use the cupboard space for a few of these ideas, below.

1   The obvious one: storage space for hoover, shopping bags, ironing board and unopened boxes of things that have moved house with you time after time.
2   Storage space for home-brew beer or wine. My brother used to brew his own beer and occasionally a bottle would pop its cork under the stairs with a muffled bloop.
3   Cosy home-office.
4   The Naughty Hole for nephews and boyfriends who misbehave.
5   Storage space for sale-bargain mistakes that are to be worn 'one day'.
6   Excess-shoe hole.
7   A halfway house between home and charity shop, for huge bin liners of old clothes, baby toys, artificial limbs and so on.
8   Home mushroom farm. Very suitable conditions. *Not on the floor* – use kits.
9   Boyfriend bundle-hole for when parents return home unexpectedly. No smoking!

❊ *Severe blushing is called idiopathic cranio-facial erythema.* ❊

How to
Light a Fire in a Grate

So your man has announced he is going to light the fire. First he shovels up a load of ashes from the grate, knocking the fire irons over noisily with his elbow and terrifying the cat. This is just by way of an overture: a flavour of what's to come.

He decides he will carry the ash outside for disposal – a shovelful at a time. As he steps gingerly across the room, the piled shovel gripped in front of him at arm's length, hot orange smuts start to fly off, landing on the rug, on the cushions, down the back of the telly. Now opening the door with one hand, the full force of the breeze catches him for the first time, blowing huge grey clouds of ash into his eyes, all over him, and back into the room. *Very loud swearing and coughing.*

Finally, he's got everything cleaned up and prepared: he's piled the kindling, put in the firelighters and artistically arranged the coals and logs over the top. Now he applies the match. One of the firelighters begins to flicker slightly and he fiddles noisily with the grate (for optimum draught). But the fire sulks. So he holds a sheet of newspaper across the opening to draw air up faster: 'Don't worry,' he reassures you, 'I know what I'm doing'. Immediately, the draught rips the paper out of his hands, sending it – a flaming ball – up the chimney.

After one or two more alarming attempts, he stands up smartly to admire his handiwork, banging his head on the mantelpiece. A single wheezy firelighter continues its heroic gasp-and-flicker performance.

It's not really that difficult. Here's how.

Required

* *3 firelighters*
* *A bunch of kindling*
* *10 lumps of coal*
* *4–5 small dry logs*
* *A box of matches*

Instructions

1 Clean the grate of ash to allow air under the fire.
2 Check your fuel is dry.
3 Arrange three firelighters on the grate amid leftover and partly burnt coals.
4 Place a bunch of kindling in a shallow wigwam over firelighters.
5 Surround with lumps of coal. These will help buttress the kindling.
6 Put some small and very dry logs over the whole arrangement, allowing huge air holes.
7 Ignite the firelighters.

8   Don't fiddle.
9   Within 15 minutes it should have taken hold. If not, check for sufficient airflow.
10 Once the kindling is flaming nicely and the small logs have taken, start bunging on more logs or coal. But don't smother.
11 And don't keep poking it. There's no point.

HINTS AND TIPS

* *Your chimney should be swept regularly*
* *Coal tends to glow but produces an intense heat*
* *Logs have jolly flames but are often not so radiantly hot*
* *A few drops of a woody essential oil on your logs a couple of hours before burning give off lovely aromas – cedar, pine and sandalwood are all good*

❋ It is considered lucky to see a chimney sweep on your wedding day. ❋

Natural Limescale Removers

Working once, as I did, in an office at the top of a Belgravia mansion, I used to get through a lot of tea. This was provided by the ancient and longtime factotum Mrs Treen, who kept a huge and elderly aluminium kettle constantly on the boil. One day I tried to lift it but it weighed a ton and when I looked inside I noticed an archaeologically significant buildup of limescale from decade upon decade of hard London water. It must have been two inches thick.

Hard water is just an informal name for water with a high mineral content, usually metal ions: mainly calcium (Ca) and magnesium (Mg) in the form of carbonates, though it may also include other metals, as well as bicarbonates and sulfates. But you don't need to know this very dull information, because you can discover your water's hardness by lathering some soap. If it produces a meagre foam, your water's hard, but if the merest scintilla makes enough froth for a movie snowstorm, then you have soft water (good for making Scotch whisky with).

Calcium carbonate (limescale) deposited on your taps is unsightly, but you can get rid of it laboriously with elbow grease, or much more easily using an entirely natural limescale remover which I'll tell you about in a moment. It's best to do this regularly because by the time it becomes as thick as the kettle I mentioned, getting it off is less a housekeeping job than a major civil engineering project.

KETTLE METHOD

Perhaps the most obvious testament to hard water is the build-up in your kettle. If you lift the lid, look inside and see a cavern of stalactitic crusts and what appear to be huge brittle ice sheets that break off and end up in your tea, then it's time to act.

1   First empty the kettle.
2   Pour in 2 inches of water and a couple of capfuls of your magic natural limescale destroyer: vinegar. Brown is fine.

3   Now for the witchcraft: boil. You *must* keep a watch, and as soon as it starts to boil switch it off. If you don't do this the vinegar will cause a noisome Vesuvian eruption, covering your worktop with an eye-watering scalding brown froth, and filling the kitchen with a mephitic effluvium.

A weekly boiling of this water-vinegar mixture in your kettle will keep it in tip-top condition. Don't forget to rinse it out after though or you'll have the vicar crossing and uncrossing his eyes and legs as he realizes there's more to today's cuppa than meets the eye.

Tap method

1   Half fill a sandwich bag with vinegar and slide it over your tap, snapping a rubber band over the lot. Leave overnight with the tap immersed in the vinegar and next morning it will be bright and shiny. Pour the vinegar down the drain; it's no good on your chips now.

Bath and shower method

1   Mix ¼ cup vinegar and 1 cup water in a spray bottle.
2   Spray bath and shower. Make sure there's nobody in there first. It's no fun being sprayed with cold Sarsons.
3   Lounge in sunshine for an hour, reading romantic novel.
4   Wipe off with wet sponge.

You need to do this regularly to make an impact. Or even better, get *someone else* to do it and go skiing instead.

❀ *More than 90% of the world's fresh water is in Antarctica.* ❀

How to
Polish a Good Table

*D*on't forget that tables – even good ones – are there to be used. I was once talking to David Linley, if you'll pardon my dropping a name, who makes lovely furniture. He said he thought tables and chairs were there to be used, which seemed hard to argue with. If they got bumped, scratched or dented, well the sun would probably rise tomorrow nonetheless. Anyway, it's not possible to have a life *and* preserve the pristine surface of your table, without wrapping it up in carpet and storing it in a crate somewhere. On the other hand, if your favourite old table is looking a bit down on its luck and you'd like to buff it up to an optimistic shine, here's how.

PREPARATION

1 Wipe and dust your table.
2 You can deal with rings and small scratches by covering them with Vaseline and leaving overnight. Wipe off the splodge next day. The broken edge of a walnut shell rubbed along an unsightly scratch will darken it.
3 Grease stains can be seen off by mixing a paste of talcum powder and methylated spirits. Apply with a brush and allow to dry. Then brush off.
4 You can get rid of old wax with a half-and-half mixture of linseed oil and genuine turpentine: smells terrific. Wipe it on with an old rag and remove it with fine steel wool. Wear rubber gloves because it does your nails no favours.

POLISHING WITH WAX

Polishing your wooden furniture with wax will bring up an attractive lustre. It is a very simple and easy process and the key to success is to use the right products. Try to find a wax polish that comes as a cream rather than a paste. It's easier to apply and won't set rock-hard. Some of the best polishes are the natural ones. Avoid those containing toluene, a malodorous poisonous solvent. It smells as if you've re-sprayed your car in the house. Use a wax containing genuine turpentine (turps). It is distilled from pine sap so its perfume is just wonderful.

REQUIRED
* *Beeswax furniture polish (specialist suppliers are easy to find)*
* *Clean cotton rags*
* *A soft lintless cloth*

INSTRUCTIONS
1   Put the wax on sparingly with a clean cotton rag, working with the grain of the wood. Don't apply huge great dollops or smear it all over ancient coatings of hardened polish. That won't glow, it will just look thicker and browner than yesterday. *See Preparation 4 above.*
2   Buff with a soft cloth that won't snag.
3   Get your friends round to admire the shine and sniff the scent.

❀ *German proverb: At a round table, every seat is the head place.* ❀

How to
Prune Roses

Petrol station flowers! There, now I've said it. What is it about blokes that makes them forget Valentine's Day, wedding anniversaries, you name it? Then at the last minute, they remember and think you won't notice when they present you with a box of wine gums and a bunch of desperate-looking flowers wrapped in the brazen cellophane of British Essoline, with the price tag still on. Nice fresh roses is what you want, proper chocolates and a bit of care and attention. You could grow roses yourself, of course, and then he could just snip a few off while watching football through the window.

Roses are cultivated round the world and are available in every colour except black and blue. But how do you prune them? Can you just cut them anywhere or what? Here's a useful guide.

Pruning is necessary to:

* Remove old and diseased wood.
* Encourage new flowering shoots.
* Keep the plant in trim, with a centre open to light and air.

The time to prune roses is during the cold weather, when the plants are dormant. Well I say that, but there were some great big yellow ones round my front door in *January* and climate change is certainly making these things harder to judge. If it's mild you can prune in November, but once frost and snow take hold put down your secateurs and wait for spring.

REQUIRED
* *A good pair of gardening or pruning gloves*
* *Some sharp secateurs*
* *A small pruning saw for big hummers*
* *Garden twine for climbers and tidying up*

INSTRUCTIONS
You need to remove any shoots that are dead, weak, spindly, old or knotty. You should also cut out shoots growing into the middle of the bush, which might produce a snarled thicket over time, along with any that are rubbing against each other.

CUTTING SHOOTS
1 Always cut just above the bud. Look for where the leaf was attached to the stem. Just above this mark is a bump. This is the bud, which will grow into a new shoot.
2 Select an outward-facing bud that will grow away from, not into, the middle of the plant.

3   Make a clean slanted cut, about ¼in above the bud. By cutting at
     an angle you will cause rain to run away from the bud, so that it
     isn't inundated.

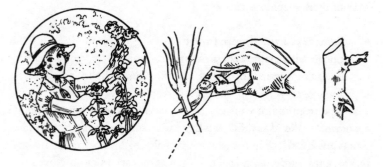

Most cultivated roses are grafted on to a vigorous, wild rose root, which
may send up 'suckers' that can overpower and kill the cultivated rose.

Suckers are light green, thin and fast growing snakey shoots, the
leaves of which look smaller than those of the cultivated rose. They
come from below the graft – where the shoots grow from the root – so
you might need to dig out some soil to reach them. Do not *cut* suckers.
Instead, pull them off at the root, which will prevent them re-growing.

Once you have pruned your roses, give them a good feed with fertilizer and homemade compost (*see* page 141).

And by the way, I know they *say* you can get black roses but they
aren't really black. Not under a good lamp anyway.

❀ *Roses are often browsed on by deer.* ❀

How to
Remove Tricky Stains
from Almost Anywhere

There's nothing quite so time consuming for the compleat housewife as clearing up after other people. Guests come round and drip
coffee on your kelim, grind ball-point pens into your Wilton, and ruin

your best shag-rugs by squashing chewing gum all over the place. Then there's clothes washing, and all the muck on the walls. If only you were rich enough to buy slaves ... Well, until that time comes, why not try some of these ingenious cleaning agents.

* *Coffee*: on carpets, apply a mixture of egg yolk and glycerin then sponge with warm water; on clothes, wash after sponging with the eggy glycerin.
* *Bird droppings on your windows*: these disappear like magic with a rag dipped in hot vinegar.
* *Sweat*: spray the dress or shirt with clear vinegar (after you've taken it off). Then wash the garment with a couple of soluble aspirins dissolved in water.
* *Ring around the collar*: try using the shampoo that's advertised as being for oily hair, and give it a good scrub with the nail brush.
* *'Orrible filthy mechanic's overalls*: soak the overalls in a can of generic cola then wash in detergent as usual.
* *Ball-point pen*: easy one if you catch it fresh. Rub the ink gently with some neat washing-up liquid then scrape the stain with a knife, and repeat.
* *Blu-tak on walls*: this is a weird one. Apply a blob of toothpaste and leave it to harden. Next day (or once it's hard) wash off the toothpaste and the Blu-tak will come with it. I do not understand how or why this works, but it seems to.
* *Scratches on a wooden table*: OK, not really a stain but can be unsightly. Rub the edges of a broken walnut shell on to the scratch. I think there's tannin in there, which darkens the wood. But don't quote me.
* *Chewing gum*: this can be a real pig. Freeze the gum with a bag of ice or frozen peas. Once it's solid, strike the gum sharply with a hammer and pick off the fractured pieces. Use a rag soaked in methylated spirits on any bits left over. Not infallible but better than nothing.

* *Residue of sticky labels on jars*: sometimes you want the jar but not the label. Peel off what you can and then use a lump of smooth peanut butter on a cotton wool ball, rubbing in circles. Or if you want to be boringly utilitarian, use methylated spirits.

* *Dust on silk flowers*: my Auntie Sarah told me about this one and it's brilliant. Put the flowers in a large paper bag and season well with plenty of salt. Now shake, and hey presto! the dust is gone. A bit like old-fashioned plain crisps. Oh dear, I'm showing my age.

❀ *Staines was the major producer of lino until the 1960s.* ❀

How to
Get the Top off
a Pickle Jar

*H*ow many times have you opened the cupboard and taken down a handsome looking jar of pickled onions, mayonnaise or whatever, and then spent 10 minutes trying – and failing – to get the top off the wretched thing?

And how peculiar it is that one's desire for something should increase in direct proportion to one's inability to get it. I'm not a huge fan of pickled walnuts as a rule but when I tried rather idly to open a jar of them one Christmas, and couldn't, I felt suddenly as if I would simply never rest until I had eaten two or three jars of them. My whole life seemed quite meaningless without a pickled walnut. It's a problem that results in an awful lot of trying everything you can think of as well as a fair bit of storming off in disgust, which is a shame really, as there is not one solution to this puzzle but several.

First, it helps to understand a bit of the science. The problem is caused during the bottling process. After the gherkins, onions or whatever go into the jar, hot vinegar follows and the lid is screwed on by a powerful machine before anything has had time to cool. As the air and liquid cool, they shrink. This means that the pressure of the air outside the jar is now greater than that inside, effectively forcing the lid on very tightly. Together with the machine-closure, and the shrinkage of the metal lid itself, this makes it a mammoth job to get the top off again.

In the old days you would just ask a man to help but some of these jars are now so huge and so ludicrously tight that even the men end up staggering around red-faced and gasping. The following tips are ones I've tried, and they've all worked for me, though you sometimes need to try more than one on a particularly contumacious container.

1   Break the vacuum seal by tapping the lid against a work surface. Not infallible this, but sometimes works.

2   Invert the jar and 'smack its bottom' hard a couple of times, just like a newborn baby. Hit and miss, this one, and more effective with narrow jars of capers or mustard pickle and that kind of thing.

3   Put the triangular tip of an old-fashioned bottle opener underneath the lid and lever it away from the glass until the vacuum is broken. You'll hear a sigh as the air escapes.

4   Use a flat screwdriver to do a similar thing. Insert it under the lid but *twist* the screwdriver to pull the lid away and release the pressure.

5   Hold the top of the jar under very hot running water for a couple of minutes, turning it so that the lid is evenly heated. This will expand the metal, and to some extent the air at the top of the jar too, allowing you to open it more easily. Just heat the lid, not the whole jar. Then try 6, 7 and 8 below.

6   Rub your hand on your thigh (or someone else's thigh if you like) for about 20 seconds. You need to be wearing jeans or something similar. Your hand will become hot and you'll get a superb grip.

7   Wrap the lid in a tea towel to give your hands more traction as you twist.

8   Wear rubber gloves to do the same job. This often helps after you've put into place a preliminary measure such as number 5, above.

9   Take a short pointy kitchen knife and in classic right-hand 'Macbeth' position, with the handle gripped firmly and the blade protruding from under your fist, bring it down with a short sharp stab on the middle of the lid. Keep your other hand out of the way. You will pierce a small hole and you'll hear a pop as the air escapes. Now twist it off: nice 'n' easy.

10 If all else fails, undo your top button and go and ask the nice man next door. Maybe he can do it and maybe he can't but what have you got to lose. *Don't* answer that.

❀ *'Paco lilla' (piccalilli) first appeared in the 18th century.* ❀

How to
Wire a Plug

Wiring a plug is another of those things that women are supposed not to be able to do. Possibly with reason: it's certainly harder if you have long fingernails. Obviously it's important to get it right so as not to burn your house down or kill the cleaner when she plugs the hoover in. The fuse (*see* illustration) will blow in most instances, saving the day, but that doesn't mean you shouldn't be careful wiring the thing. Here are the instructions in a nutshell. They are designed for modern plugs not those ancient bakelite things with wires of mystery colours like red and black. Get a professional to tackle those.

INSTRUCTIONS

1   Take the plug apart. This is often where the O-level cursing starts. You can spend hours fiddling about with table knives, coins and

nail files before deciding on a proper screwdriver. And even then it can be a nuisance. Who designed these nutty contraptions?

2 Using a sharp penknife (or similar) cut around the outer cable sheathing and strip off about 1½ins to expose the coloured wires.

3 Cut around and peel off the insulation from each wire – using your knife to expose roughly ½in of the metal core.

4 Dealing with each wire in turn, twist its strands neatly together.

5 Connect the wires to their proper terminals. The brown or 'live' wire goes into the little hole in the terminal on the fuse holder marked 'L'. Screw it down tight so that it's secure. As you do this the fuse will probably fall out and roll under the fridge and the fuse holder will come apart in your hands. Time for some A-level swearing. Retrieve and replace the fuse. Now screw the blue 'neutral' wire into the little hole on the terminal marked 'N'. finally secure the green-and-yellow 'earth' wire to the terminal at the top marked 'E' or ⏚. An easy way to remember this is: bLue Left, bRown Right. Instead of a little hole on the terminals, some plugs have a little screw-down arrangement. Just wrap the wire round the axis and tighten securely, making sure no bits of wire are trailing or sticking out. Be certain that the insulation reaches right up to the terminal. OK it's all very fiddly – a few undergraduate expletives will help.

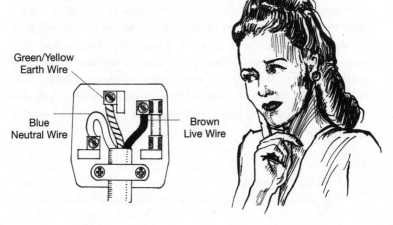

Green/Yellow
Earth Wire

Blue
Neutral Wire

Brown
Live Wire

6   Some appliances – marked 🔲 – do not have an earth wire be-
     cause they are double insulated, with no exposed metal parts. In
     this case you can just forget the earth terminal.
7   Make sure the flex is in position and tighten the cord-grip over
     the cable's outer sheath. Another fiddly job.
8   If there's no fuse or the fuse needs replacing, read the instructions
     on the device to see what rating of fuse it takes and put the proper
     one in. If the appliance works at 3A (amps), use a 5A fuse. If the
     device works at 10A, use a 13A fuse.
9   Screw on the plug cover. Sometimes the screw that does this job
     is just too short so that you have to squeeze the cover on while
     screwing, alternately pinching your skin and dropping the cover.
     Some proper postgraduate blasphemy is what's required here.
     Followed by a stiff drink.

❀ *The first electric toaster was unveiled in 1905.* ❀

How to
Make a Mateus Rosé Shell Lamp

S ophistication was epitomized in the 1970s by that unique article of
interior design, the Mateus Rosé shell lamp. In case this is something you haven't come across before, let me fill you in. Mateus Rosé
is a Portuguese wine that comes in a bottle like a short-necked sitar.
After being evacuated of wine these were often covered in small
seashells, and a light fitting and lampshade were then attached, or else
an especially drippy candle was stuck in the neck resulting in a wax
sculpture that was irresistible to pick at during a fondue evening. This
is how to make one if you ever come over all retro.

REQUIRED
*   *A Mateus Rosé bottle*
*   *Enough shells to go round: a mix of sizes, shapes and colours*

* *Araldite (this is not the Greek God of something but a kind of epoxy resin they glue aeroplanes together with)*
* *An electric light-fitting with flex*
* *A lamp shade*

INSTRUCTIONS

1 Drink wine, peel off labels and wash bottle.
2 Check that electric light fitting goes in top of bottle OK. Why not take the bottle when you buy the fitting?
3 Because the glue hardens quickly you will have to decorate your bottle in 2-inch-square areas, a little at a time, rather like Michelangelo doing a fresco. Sort the shells so you have enough for each bit you are working on. Don't use all the best ones first – that is a beginner's mistake that results in a nice bit on one side and cracked old rubbishy shells everywhere else. Save a few small-ish ones for going up the neck. Even damaged shells can be used if they are stuck nice-side out.
4 Mix the glue and apply to an area at the bottom of the bottle. Work in small zones a couple of inches high till you have gone all the way round. If you want a ringed effect then you should work in ascending hoops with shells of a contrasting size or colour in alternating hoops. If you want random coverage then just work on a patch at a time. A horrid alternative look may be achieved by using a sort of white chewing gum-type adhesive that squidges round the shells so that they are embedded rather than daintily stuck on.
5 Allow everything to dry.
6 Push the light fitting into the top of the bottle, undo the top plastic ring, place lamp shade on, replace plastic ring and put in bulb.
7 Invite chap round for mellow evening.

❋ *The oldest US lightbulb has been burning since 1901.* ❋

How to
Make Tea for a Builder

*H*ow to make tea for a tradesman is one of those black arts that they don't teach you at school or Girl Guides; you are just supposed to know how to do it by some sort of tannic osmosis. This is unfortunate, since getting it wrong can foul up an otherwise fruitful and happy relationship, resulting in unputtied windows falling out, untidied debris causing accidents, unvarnished doors warping in the rain and unpointed brickwork letting in the damp. So it's important to get it right. In the words of the old Chinese proverb: look after your builder and your builder will look after you.

But while you should look after your builder's tea needs, you must not overindulge him. Otherwise he'll end up sitting there texting his girlfriend or reading the *Sun* while you buzz around, bringing his pipe and slippers and making his dinner. So here are a few guidelines that will keep you on the straight and narrow.

* Before the building work starts, lay in serious amounts of sugar. Four or five sacks of the stuff is probably about right for a week's building work. Never get anything fancy (brown). Very bright white refined sugar is the only type that counts.

* The perfect recipe combines nine parts sugar to one part boiling water, with teabag. The proper way to prepare it is to boil the water and pour over one or two teabags in a large (if possible, indestructible) mug. Then pour in the sugar and do your best to stir. Do not give a builder any item of crockery that you value. The more you value it the more likely he is to knock its handle off or absentmindedly mix up turps and linseed oil in it. Some builders like to receive the tea with the bag and spoon still in so they can squeeze out the last drops against the side of the mug. If you do this, you'll find the spoon will stand upright, supported by the density of the liquid.

* Any type of tea that comes in a fancy box, smells of lemons or

oranges or train tunnels or cat's pee will be completely unacceptable to a proper builder and will be poured into pot plants or down drains. And your card will be marked.

* Make the tea at regular times but not too frequently.

* Accompany the tea with a good dunking biscuit (HobNobs are good dunkers, as are ginger nuts. Bourbons and custard creams are really overtime biscuits and should be reserved for special occasions such as after the final clean-up or the topping out ceremony.)

* Never offer tea or biscuits before your builders have actually done any work. You should, however, alert them early on, in Pavlovian style, that tea will be provided mid-morning, when you will also, 'take the opportunity to see how things are going'. Putting it this way shows your solicitude but also hints at a steely determination to make sure they are on the case and doing what they should be doing. You are conditioning them to the idea of reward for performance and, by inference, also to the possibility of the withholding of privileges. A look up the ladder at 11, with the question, 'How are you getting on and are you ready for a cup of tea?' lets them know that the tea is somehow dependent on progress. This is called psychology.

* Tea should be served no more than three times a day. Otherwise you'll be paying for them to drink tea and munch biscuits for more than half an hour of their working day. The minute you suspect slackness or overindulgence, let them know: 'Oh, I thought you were going to finish this wall by 11. Sorry I'm obviously holding things up with too many tea

breaks. I'll come back at 4 o'clock.' This is called employee communication.

* Don't bother with a teapot – this isn't the Duchess of Royston you're entertaining and it will score you no points.

❀ *A 1999 study found tea drinkers have a 44% lower risk of heart attack.* ❀

How to
Make a Sausage Dog Draught-Excluder

*B*efore central heating the wind used to come under doors like a knife to such an extent that Thomas Hardy wrote of footprints in the snow which had blown into his entrance hall through the gap. Brrrrrrr! I'm surprised he didn't sit straight down and write *The Mayor of Casterfridge*. (I don't often make jokes.)

I'm puzzled why Hardy didn't make himself a sausage dog draught excluder. They aren't exactly difficult and you could easily knock one up between chapters or poems. There are two main versions: the lazy 'mongrel' type and the deluxe 'pedigree'.

REQUIRED
* *All your usual sewing stuff*
* *Loads of rags*
* *Other materials variously specified below, which I won't bore you by repeating*

INSTRUCTIONS (LAZY)
1 Take one leg of a pair of woollen tights or a thick (hideous) lyle stocking – 60 denier. (In case you are unaware, 'denier' is nothing to do with Holocaust denial; it's a unit of measurement for the linear mass density of fibres defined as the mass in grams per 9,000 metres. Any the wiser? Me neither.)

2   Mend any holes (not the one you put your leg in, obviously).
3   Cut up old rags, ancient tea towels, dead cushions etc.
4   Stuff the stocking full.
5   Sew up the top and that's it.

INSTRUCTIONS (DELUXE)

1   Get hold of a nice, large, piece of heavy velvet.
2   Measure the width of your draughty door and cut a rectangle just
    a little longer and about 10ins across.
3   Fold in half along its length, *inside out*, and sew up one of the
    short edges and the long edge to make a tube, open at one end.
4   Evert the tube (turn right-side out) and stuff with kapok. Put
    plenty in so that it's nice and firm and attractively round, with no
    unsightly bumps or hollows.
5   Hand sew the last seam by folding the cut edges inside and care-
    fully oversewing.
6   You can leave the thing like a sausage or cover it in sequins or
    chenille blobs or whatever you like. But if you want it to really
    look like a dog then make a little stuffed head from matching
    material, add buttons for eyes and nose, give it some nice floppy
    velvety ears and a tail, and four tiny little legs, one at each corner.
    Another good use for the spare fishnet stocking (*see* page 105) is
    as a string vest for Rover. Doesn't he look sweet? That's rhetori-
    cal, please don't burden me with your stories about how it's all
    gone wrong. Let's face it, I have my own problems.

Should the gale coming under your door be unusually strong, sew a
heavy chain into the thing before you stuff it.

❀ *Many dachshunds suffer back problems.* ❀

How to
Make and Plant a Trailing Bin Liner

When I was a student, I spent some time in lodgings with a land-lady called Mrs Golda Gertler, who was enthusiastically Jewish. And though she didn't bother talking shop with me, one of her Gentile lodgers, she did spend many hours on the landing, bending the ears of her Jewish 'guests'. The subject was often the Six-Day War, on which she seemed to be an authority.

The tenant of flat 5, an itinerant arbitrager called Bobby Bernheim, said he habitually dropped bread pudding into Mrs Gertler's piano when she'd harangued him for longer than he could bear. I think it was he who told me she had once arranged a private meeting with the Chief Rabbi and that after an hour of muttering voices from the other side of a closed door the Rabbi's secretary finally heard the plaintive cry: 'But Madam, I'm *already* Jewish!'

Mrs Gertler often got things a bit wrong. I recall her once saying about a neighbour in a fur coat: 'Look at her, all dressed up in her refinery,' and she used to refer quite often to what she termed, 'the hanging baskets of Babylon'.

Hanging baskets are tricky. Easier is the trailing bin liner. Here's the proper way.

INSTRUCTIONS

1   Lay a good quality bin liner on the ground, short ends at the sides, and tape the open end closed.

2   You are now gong to make an open tube with a diameter one quarter of its height. Imagine wrapping the bin liner round a seven-inch-diameter pipe, taping it down and sliding it off. You'd be left with an open tube with parallel sides, seven inches across its mouth and 28 inches high (the original width of the bag). To do this without the benefit of the imaginary pipe, fold one end of

the bag across ²/₃ of the way, fold over the remaining third and tape down the ends, outside and in.

3   To close the bottom, tie off the end securely with twine and trim the surplus plastic so that you have a sort of rough floppy bucket.

4   Pack this tightly with potting compost, your favourite nutrients and water-retaining crystals.

5   Tie off the top, leaving a small hole for watering.

6   Make very small holes in the side, one for each plant you will put in, and use tiny 'plug' plants. *Note*: push the roots *up* into the soil, not down.

7   Plant up the sides of the bin liner and put a couple of good danglers in the top so that they sprout near the twine. Use wow-factor flowers such as lobelia, small petunias (million bells), violas, ivy, busy Lizzy, and verbena.

8   Amazingly, when the plants have got going, there will be no bin liner showing, it will just be a floral profusion on a string.

9   *Never let it dry out.*

10   Feed regularly with a liquid fertilizer.

11   Dead head regularly to encourage new flowers.

12   Enter for the Chelsea show.

❀   *The bin liner was invented in 1950 by three men, including Frank Plomp.*   ❀

How to
Sound Like You Know What You're Talking About at the Butcher's

*T*hese days, it's quite a job to find a butcher who remembers your name and seems to know what he's talking about. I'm lucky, there's one near me who does the butchering right there in front of you and it's a joy to watch. The problem is that the supermarkets have cured us of our knowledge so that it can be hard to know what to ask for when you enter a *real* butcher's.

Here's a short glossary of some of the more interesting cuts to give you a head start.

OFFAL

* *Haggis*: sheep's stomach stuffed with boiled liver, heart, lungs, rolled oats and other stuff. Delicious!
* *Faggots*: minced pork (mainly liver and cheek), bread, herbs and onion wrapped in a pig's caul. Ooer!
* *Brawn*: leftover pork meat from the skull. Set in gelatin and chilled. Ugh!
* *Tripe*: white honeycomb-like stuff made from the first three of a cow's four stomachs. Yikes!
* *Chitterlings*: pig's intestinal pipes. Bleurgh!

PORK

* *Neck*: the best part of the neck is used in sausage meat.
* *Shoulder*: boned and rolled makes a roasting joint. Can also be diced or minced.
* *Loin*: best for pork chops. Also cured to make back bacon.
* *Belly*: fatty but makes a superb roast or stew if well prepared.
* *Knuckle or shank end*: boned and rolled for roasting.

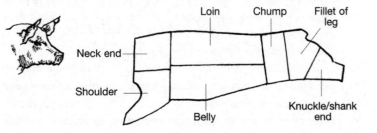

BEEF

* *Neck*: minced for shepherd's pie or hamburgers.
* *Shoulder*: stews and casseroles.
* *Shin*: a versatile meat for shepherd's pie etc.
* *Brisket*: needs to be cooked slowly.
* *Sirloin and fillet*: prime, marbled, juicy roasting joints and steaks. Fillet is actually part of the sirloin. Very tender but less flavoursome than rump.
* *Rump*: the joint next to the sirloin. Delicious for kebabs.
* *Topside and silverside*: good for roasting.
* *Leg*: best in pies and casseroles.

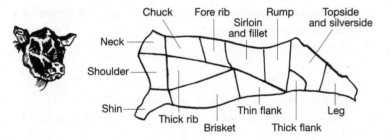

LAMB

* *Shoulder*: boned and rolled or can be cut into chops.
* *Scrag end of neck*: delicious for stewing.
* *Best end of neck*: a joint with a row of half a dozen ribs (rack of lamb). Two joined together and arranged bones-out, with little chef's hats on, are the famous crown of lamb. Also sold as chops with one rib each.
* *Loin and chump*: divided into loin end and chump end and cut into chops – chump has a round bone and loin has a T-bone – or you can roast in one piece.
* *Leg*: can be bought whole or split into two joints, fillet and shank. Lamb shank can be on or off the bone. It is a delicious succulent roasting joint and one of my favourites.

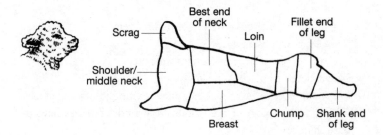

The less fashionable (cheaper) cuts are nowadays reclaiming the attention they deserve. Longer, slower cooking times for 'Cinderellas' such as brisket of beef, trotters or belly of pork produce some of the most delicious meals imaginable. If in doubt about what to go for ask your butcher – he knows.

❀ *Shari Lewis's Lamb Chop 'sock-puppet' has appeared on TV since 1957.* ❀

III

The Perfect Hostess

How to turn heads, charm the birds from the trees, and be the hostess with the mostest

Serve dinner backwards, do anything, but for goodness' sake, do something weird.

ELSA MAXWELL

How to
Be the Hostess with
the Mostest

*H*ardly anyone I know has time to entertain in the way people used to, once upon a long time ago. These days we are constantly flying around the home picking up after other people, or flying out of the door at 6.30 to earn a crust and flying home again at 9.30 to gobble a takeaway in front of the telly with a bottle of Cava. Our children are raised by nannies, our dogs walked by walkers and we hardly have time for our friends, who seem almost as busy as ourselves. So the idea of a dinner party or a cocktail party or any kind of ghastly entertainment in our own home seems like more trouble than it's worth. But don't despair, because I have some top tips to make entertaining easy. It's rather like making a film:

* *Actor/director*: don't just direct the action, you should be part of the story too. Although gourmet food is delicious you want to enjoy the company of your guests and they have no desire to see you in yellow Marigolds and a pinny ferrying dishes to and fro all night. So take time to talk to your guests, join in the fun and relax a bit. Most of the hard work should be over once they arrive (*see Catering* below).

* *Assistant directors*: your assistant directors can be close friends or family. They can take coats, order cabs, hand round bowls of nuts, show people where the loo is, shoo smokers on to the patio, and so on.

* *Cast*: cast your guests as if for a blockbuster. This means a mix of people, with a good sprinkling of extroverts. Not boors – extroverts. If it's sit-down don't put couples together, share them out. And don't invite people you hate.

* *Catering*: preparation is the single most important element of a successful do. Plan ahead and prepare as much food as you can so

you're not stuck in the kitchen all night. Here's a secret: guests don't really care what they eat so long as it isn't actually poisonous. They've come to see you and to relax a bit. Remember that Bridget Jones girl making blue soup by mistake? We've all done that sort of thing and guests don't mind so long as you can turn it into an entertainment. Keep some emergency stuff in the freezer and in the cupboard in case of disaster. It needs to be instantly do-able though.

Tinned consommé is a fantastic starter that's easy to keep at serving temperature in a giant pan till you're ready. Just pour in a capful of sherry two minutes before serving and they will swear the soup's home-made. Bangers and mash is a real winner for gentlemen, whether it's sit-down or buffet. It's easy to cook in advance and keeps hot for absolutely ages. Buy really good (expensive) sausages though. The more meat they have in them the less they will shrink. Provide a huge jug of piping-hot gravy (I use royal game soup for my gravy: it's unbeatable and very quick, just open the tins and heat). The smells of warming consommé and gravy are delicious wafting from the kitchen as your guests arrive. You can also fry some garlic in butter if you like – not for eating, it just smells good. Vegetarians can be catered for with a good cheese flan, which you can make or buy. But if you buy it, remove it from its wrappings and surround it with a load of fresh rocket and chopped sweet cherry tomatoes as a disguise.

For pudding, I suggest buying some fancy cakes, or a big fruit-cake and slicing it up in huge chunks in advance. Put it on plates and microwave for thirty seconds before serving, with a huge jug of single cream or some decent ice cream. Vast pots of coffee are easy and you can serve it with some of those continental biscuits. They always go down a treat. Get the idea? Very little faffing around in the kitchen, good food that people imagine you made yourself, and therefore plenty of time to spend with your guests. Don't give guests anything you haven't tested on yourself first though. They don't like to be guinea pigs.

* *Plot and dialogue*: seat poets next to accountants and introduce women to men. An introvert will blossom if put next to a warm and friendly person. Don't dump two shy people together or they will stare at their shoes with a rictus of shame and the frost will spread round the whole room. When you do introduce two people, help them to get talking by saying something such as: 'Susie, this is Malcolm who is an expert on the flesh-eating disease, necrotizing fasciitis. Malcolm, Susie collects glass spiders.' Then circulate. I knew a *hostess with the mostest* who used to run dinner parties with a theme, or where people had to guess what the name was on the sticker on their head as soon as they arrived. I never enjoyed her dos very much.

* *Set*: parties in offices are horrible for lots of reasons: the bottom photocopying, the stock cupboard groping, the large numbers of people you loathe. But they are certainly not helped by the buzzing fluorescent lights. Keep your own lighting at a level where people can see their food, fags and each other's faces but not so low they are searching for doorways with their out-stretched hands. Christmas lights can turn a dull patio into an intimate twinkling fairyland: especially if your guests have had a couple of drinks.

Flowers are always a winner. A restaurant with flowers on the table can get away with another tenner on the bill, it is said. Put fresh flowers all over. Unless you are entertaining the National Hayfever Convention, of course.

A small gift for each guest at the dinner table, such as a wooden toy, modelling balloons, a mouth organ, a book of poems is a nice touch. Suit your gifts to the guests. If you know them well you can really please people by providing something inexpensive but personal, whether it be a plectrum, some chocolates, a packet of sparklers or a cigar.

* *Wrap*: the best guests will leave at a decent hour wishing they could have stayed longer as they wave you good night. Some, however, will sit rooted to the sofa until cockcrow – unless you do something. Don't worry about offending them; they are always insensitive. Yawning and stretching is a good start, followed by putting on your nightie. If they are still there when you come down, take out one of those loudhalers they use on marches, and announce: 'Earth calling the Wilsons – it's time to go home!' That ought to do it.

❀ *'My vigor, vitality and cheek repel me.' Lady Nancy Astor.* ❀

How to
Entertain Unexpected Guests

*T*here's a lovely story about Johnny Speight, who invited Frankie Howerd round for dinner and then forgot all about it till he saw him coming up the garden path. Leaping from his armchair, Speight ordered his wife into the kitchen to improvise a meal. 'But I haven't been shopping,' she protested. 'Never mind: do your best,' he hissed as the bell rang. Bacon and eggs isn't much of a dinner if you've been expecting a spread, and when it was presented to him Howerd stared for a moment and then expostulated: 'This isn't dinner. It's *breakfast*.'

OK, there's a difference between forgotten and unexpected guests, but not much, in the sense that you've got to extemporize a bit. Here are some tips for dealing with the unexpected sort.

If they are guests you are happy to see:

* Make it clear what they can expect: if you're going out at 6, let them know.
* If you are busy when they turn up try to involve them. Get them out in the garden with you or ask them to help you prepare the food.
* Never apologize for the mess. In fact, there's no need to apologize for anything – it's your house.
* Make sure they don't feel they have put you to huge trouble, unless they have.
* Put the kettle on straight away (does it suit you?).

* Don't keep thinking about the final episode of the costume drama that you've been waiting all week to watch. Keep the telly off!

* Always maintain emergency supplies in the house so you can make a throw-together meal at any time: soup, pasta, beans and a few tins of interesting stuff. In fact spaghetti with a jar of (emergency) sauce and some bits and bobs hurled in will make a feast in a flash. Especially if you unplug a bottle of wine at the same time. Frying an onion always produces a homely aroma and makes people feel welcome.

* If there are children in tow, do something exciting with them, such as playing a game. A good one is to see who can cram the most grapes under their lips and then whistle without laughing. There will be grapes on the floor, I'm afraid, so invite everyone to play outside. (Not in the main road, obviously.)

* If there's no food in the house, order a takeaway and suggest splitting the bill.

* Go for a long walk with the dog and catch up on your visitors' news. You definitely need to have a dog for this one, girls. Walking around with an empty lead makes you look too strange.

If they are unwanted guests try the following:

* Pretend to be out. But don't get caught through the window, hiding behind the sofa. Very embarrassing.

* Ask them to help you drain the radiators.

* Serve them sardine custard with chopped eels and fish lips.

* Show them your lifetime's accumulation of holiday snaps. Even the most hardened bores will find this too much to bear.

* Turn on the gas taps and go out. At least you'll be able to call the blackened ruins of your home your own, when you return.

 ❀ The Day the Earth Caught Fire *(1961) was directed by Val Guest.* ❀

How to
Mix a Harvey Wallbanger

Why must cocktails have such ridiculous names? I feel daft enough asking for a Screwdriver but the epithets attached to some recent drinks are simply unspeakable in polite company. Then there's 'cocktail' itself, where on earth did that come from? I'll tell you: it first appeared in the May 13 1806 issue of the American *Balance and Columbia Repository* where, in response to a reader's query, it was defined as: 'A potent concoction of spirits, bitters, water, and sugar.' Did the editor of *Balance and Columbia Repository*, I wonder, make it up?

My favourite story about the origins of the Harvey Wallbanger is this one. A Californian surfer called Harvey liked his Screwdrivers enlivened with Galliano – a delicious liqueur containing anise, lavender and mint as well as vanilla, cinnamon and coriander. (You can get it in most supermarkets.) One unhappy night, after losing a big surfing competition, Harvey drowned his sorrows so comprehensively that his several abortive attempts to find the bar's exit resulted in his head making repeated contact with the wall. And a name was born.

My least favourite, probably true, story is that bartender Bill Doner just invented it. Anyway, here's the way to make it.

INGREDIENTS
* *1 part vodka*
* *4 parts orange juice*
* *2tsps Galliano*
* *6 ice cubes*
* *1 orange slice*

INSTRUCTIONS
There are five main methods for mixing cocktails: layering, building, blending, shaking and stirring. You will recall that James Bond prefers his Martini cocktails shaken not stirred. This is because you get a different

blend, temperature and appearance with methods of different sorts. This procedure for mixing a Harvey Wallbanger is a combination of layering and shaking. Shaking ensures that the drink is chilled and diluted to the proper degree, and of course it's entertaining to watch.

1   Put three ice cubes, the vodka and the orange juice into a cocktail shaker.
2   Shake well for 30 seconds. Try to look the part.
3   Strain into a tall glass over the rest of the ice, leaving the shaken ice in the shaker.
4   Float the Galliano over the top. This looks very cool and is not hard to accomplish. What you do is carefully pour the Galliano over the back of a spoon that is touching the surface of the drink.
5   Decorate with slices of orange.
6   Serve to the lounge lizard in the white tux. No cocktail umbrellas please.

❀ *November 8 is Harvey Wallbanger Day.* ❀

How to
Pack the Perfect Picnic Hamper

*T*here can't have been many songwriters more successful than the prolific Jimmy Kennedy. What do you mean you've never heard of him? *If you go down to the woods today you're in for a big surprise.* That was one of his lines, from the million-selling *Teddy Bears' Picnic*, and he wrote numerous others you'll have heard of. Which leads me to my sermon for today: how to pack the perfect picnic hamper. Naturally it's as easy as pie (pork) to pack an imperfect hamper. Often things are missing: there's no knife to spread the butter or there's no bottle opener for the beer, or there's no salt for the boiled eggs. So, if you'd like to do it properly, grab your hamper because here's the inside know-how.

Instructions

1   Get yourself a decent receptacle to start off with. It doesn't have to be a handmade Victorian wicker thing with leather straps, but neither will half a dozen plastic shopping bags do.

2   Make a list of what you need first and set it all out so you can tick it off, one item at a time, as it goes into the basket.

3   Don't go mad with the contents. Mrs Beeton, bless her tongs, used to insist on a gigantic list of essentials, including a stick of horseradish, a little ice, some lump sugar, some pounded sugar, a bottle of well-corked mint sauce, *four* teapots and *three* corkscrews. She must have belonged to the militant wing of the party. Who carried all that impedimenta anyway – Mr Beeton? No, keep it to a minimum, but don't omit anything vital. (Usually it's the salt that gets left behind, ruining the entire meal.)

4   Bring *enough* plates, cutlery, cups and glasses.

5   Some sandwich bags are a good idea. You can mix things in them, drop apple cores in, and so on.

6   Food that doesn't need cutlery is good: sausages, pork pies, boiled eggs, pickles, sandwiches, celery and carrots, fruitcake, chicken

wings, tearable bread like focaccia or baguettes – oh! My mouth's watering already.

7   If you must take a tin of something, for goodness' sake bring the tin opener or your name will be mud (*see salt* above).

8   Don't forget the condiments: chutney, pepper, pickles, mustard, etc. These can turn a boring Scotch egg, chicken leg or cocktail sausage into a feast fit for a queen.

9   Salads must be robust. Thin lettuce, cucumber and soft tomatoes can turn to mush on the way. I often combine the thickly sliced veggies in a big container and refine the chunks in situ, adding salad dressing on arrival.

10   Cheddar sweats like a stevedore when it gets warm. Try Stilton, which can survive the heat of a nuclear explosion.

11   For puds, avoid jam and other very sticky hard-to-manage sugary drippers because of the wasps: cup cakes, fruit and berries are all OK and you can dip almost anything into a pot of double cream.

12   If you want cold drinks, put a few cans or plastic bottles in the freezer for an hour or so before you leave (some careful experiment required). By the time you arrive, they will be just right. Saves lugging ice around. I always take sugarless drinks: avoids the wasps and doesn't home in on my thighs either. Spritzers can be made on site and any kind of cold bubbles are good.

Finally, bring a few plastic shopping bags for the rubbish. I don't know about you, but I always seem to produce a ton of rubbish on my picnics. Here are a few of the other obvious things that sometimes get forgotten.

*   *A decent rug. There's nothing worse than lunch surrounded by cow pats and thistles.*
*   *A couple of cushions*
*   *Plenty of water*
*   *A bottle opener that will do wine and beer. This is important*

* *A sharp knife (vital)*
* *Some hand wipes. These are a boon for impromptu dish wiping as well as hand and face cleaning.*
* *A roll of kitchen paper (gets used a lot)*
* *Paper or linen napkins*
* *Sun hats or a gigantic parasol that will also keep the rain off*
* *THE SALT!*

⊛ *'Picnic' comes from the French,* pique-nique. ⊛

How to
Dance with a Man Shorter than Yourself

*D*on't look down your nose at short men if you are a lady of stature; it's possible to be *short*, dark and handsome. Alexander the Great and Napoleon were both small, after all, but that didn't top them being powerful and attractive, while Tom Cruise is diminutive (5ft 7ins), rich *and* good-looking. Finally, think of the famous English variety comedian Jimmy Clitheroe, who was only 4ft 3ins and had a squeaky voice and looked ridiculous and wasn't funny. Well, OK, let's forget Jimmy Clitheroe. But the others are all right.

So while it's true that more children are fathered by tall men than short ones, and that short men are more likely to be poor, fat, fag-smoking heart attacks waiting to happen, there's no reason you shouldn't be able to dance with a Toulouse-Lautrec-size chap even if you're lofty, elegant and poised like Tom Cruise's ex-missus Nicole Kidman (just short of 6ft), who managed OK.

When it comes down to it, you can deal with the problem of dancing with a man who is shorter than you by two methods, known as *go with it*, and *even out the difference*.

The *go with it* camp is probably more likely to contain cheerful normal ladies, while the *even out the differencers* are never going to be really happy – a bit like Prince Charles when they made him stand on that crate for the royal photograph of him and his wife. No wonder he had that funny look on his face.

Go with it

Going with it is so much easier than evening out the difference because there's only so much leaning and flat-shoe-wearing you want to be doing if you're statuesque. Why hide your height under a bushel? If you've got it, *flaunt it*. So remember:

* Never take your shoes off; perhaps wear a low heel but only if this doesn't compromise your own looks – if you don't make much of the difference, neither will others.
* Concentrate on each other, not what other people may be thinking.
* If he is a lot shorter than you, be sure your nipple camouflage is in good order; it will be up for very close and extended scrutiny.

Even out the difference
Here are a few tips:

* Use perspective to your advantage by keeping a distance between yourselves. This greatly reduces the possibility of a slow smooch though.
* Flat shoes for you, built up shoes for him.
* Hair down.
* Tangos are good because of all that bending over backwards.
* Train him to wear stilts under his trousers (you're getting desperate).

❀ *General Tom Thumb was 3ft 4ins tall.* ❀

How to
Perfume a Room in 10 Seconds

Once upon a time I was looking round houses in search of a suitable one to buy. This can be a demoralizing process at the best of times because (A) you realise that what you can afford is smaller and nastier than you'd at first imagined, and (B) many of the places you are shown are dumps. I remember one house where there were hideous specimens of a man's pants scattered all over a Black-Hole-of-Calcutta bedroom, and another where a jam doughnut adhered mysteriously to the ceiling of an otherwise charming Georgian property. Further places smelled of dogs or damp – which leads me on to the subject of today's life-coaching seminar.

There can be many reasons why you wish to perfume a room in a hurry, from the desire to create a welcoming aroma for sudden visitors, to the need to cloak the odour of yesterday's bubble and squeak, or the requirement that your feculent bedsit be swiftly converted into a cosy concubine's lair.

Let us forget for the moment the nose-cauterizingly pungent commercial preparations that you can nowadays plug into the wall, and those aerosol products that 'neutralize odours'. These will conjure up for any visitor a baleful redolence of the eye-watering pong you get from those plastic things that turn the water blue in your toilet, or the noisome miasmatic stink of fake pineapple that lurks over the sewage farm near Gatwick Airport on a hot day.

For olfactory cheerfulness, try some of these quick fixes.

* Spray a few lightbulbs with perfume and switch them on. Instantaneous and strong in effect.
* Drop essential oil on to a cotton wool ball and tuck it behind a radiator.
* Mix about 20 drops of lemongrass or lavender oil with water in a plant mister and spray it around. A subtle effect, best on hot days.
* Lilies, freesias, hyacinths and other flowers give off a powerful

aroma. But unless you've got them in the place already, they're hardly quick.

* If a fire is burning, drop woody oils like cedar or sandalwood on to a log before burning. Alternatively drop oils on the hot tiles round the fire.

* If you are a bit of a hippy, just light a joss stick.

* In an emergency, set light to a spill of brown paper. This will successfully mask even the mashing of a stinkhorn.

* Cut or peel oranges, tangerines or other citrus fruit for a subtler effect.

* Fry onions or garlic. This is good for concealing old cooking smells and giving guests an appetite.

* Light a huge cigar and blow it about. Very fast effect but rather lacking in femininity.

* Open the Camembert.

❀ *The grandiose Imperial Majesty perfume costs £1,234 a bottle.* ❀

How to
Curtsy

Just in case you don't know, the word 'curtsy' is a variation of 'courtesy'. The action itself is a formal greeting (made exclusively by girls and women), in which you bend your knees with one foot in front of the other and do a little bob, sometimes holding your skirt (doesn't look so good in jeans). It was once used by servants in front of their employers and by sugar-and-spice-type girls to grownups in suits but is used almost exclusively these days to show reverence towards members of the royal family.

Nonetheless, in these more egalitarian times, demonstrations of deference to mere authority are falling into disuse and the curtsy is on its last legs. Since 2003 for example, at the request of the Duke and Duchess of Kent, exhausted female tennis players have no longer been required to curtsy when they stagger off Wimbledon's Centre Court. As transvestite necrophile Norman Bates says in *Psycho*: 'One by one you drop the formalities.'

But there again you never know when a curtsy is going to come in handy, for example, at one of those embassy dos where liveried waiters are flourishing the Ambassador's gilded plate-spiled high with pyramids of those chocolate balls in a bit of foil. Or at your coming-out party of course.

INSTRUCTIONS

1 Unlike the 'bob' curtsy, the quintessentially old-fashioned deep curtsy requires you to 'slide back' on the inclined right foot, curling it behind and around the left, which remains static throughout.

2 Your sliding foot takes your weight, allowing you to sink gracefully, finally coming to rest, sitting on your bent right leg, arms falling to the side and head lowered. This is a highly submissive and vulnerable pose.

3 When you are ready to stand, take your weight on your left foot, rising to your full height again. This deep curtsy is the basis of the modern curtsies you will have seen or done, even the cheeky little ones.

A weird variation of this deep curtsy requires you to bend the knees outwards, akimbo-style instead of curling the right leg around the left. I've never tried this one but it sounds ungainly to me, as if you were lowering yourself perpendicularly on to a space hopper without the benefit of hands.

By the seventeenth century a hierarchy of curtsies had developed indicating varying levels of deference and I have set out below the three main curtsy types.

THREE TYPES OF CURTSY

* *Curtsy en avant (literally, 'ahead')*: this one, used on entering a room, looks to me like the old servant's-bob curtsy, where you slide either foot to the front and then bend at the knees, body straight and weight equally distributed. You rise supporting your weight on the front foot.
* *Curtsy en arriere (literally 'behind')*: recommended for use on leaving a room, you step to the side and curtsy but with your weight supported on the back foot.
* *Curtsy en passant (in passing)*: useful as a repeatable curtsy in a reception line. In this one you position yourself next to the person you are greeting, making a step on the left foot and half turn towards him or her. You then bend your knees, bringing the right foot forward. You rise with your weight on the same foot.

Or you could just say hello like a normal person.

❀ *Cherie Blair's refusal to curtsy is said to have amused the Queen.* ❀

How to
Tell When a Man Fancies You

Women are so far ahead of men in the field of understanding and using body language that they are already at a distinct advantage. Men, bless them, are about as clever in this department as a gibbon trying to get a fistful of raisins out of a narrow jam jar. That is to say, not very. Men are also simpler than women, fancying almost all of them almost all of the time and giving out fairly obvious signals. If you can spot these signals you will be ahead of the blonde, blue-eyed, big-boobed competition – always a good thing. You should therefore start from the assumption that Man A *does*, in fact, fancy you. Your problem will be the common female one of Man A passing *your* acceptability tests. How complicated it all is. Anyway, let's not go into that but get straight on with things.

WHAT TO LOOK OUT FOR.

*   *Erect posture*: the first sign that a chap is taking an interest in you is that he will pull in his gut, stand or sit up more erect and puff out his chest. He will do these things without realizing.

*   *Preening*: just like those birds on the Discovery Channel, men go in for preening. Tie straightening is a giveaway, as is hair smoothing, cufflink tinkering, clothes brushing and so forth.

*   *Body position*: if he turns his body towards you that's a positive sign. A more subtle sign is if he points his foot or feet towards you. Sometimes when trying to conceal his interest in you from someone (his wife?) he will not turn towards you but will subconsciously point his foot in your direction. If you spot this, you will notice that every now and then he also glances at you. If he does, smile warmly or wink – depending on what you think you can get away with. This should cause steam to rise from his trousers.

*   *Present buying*: if he buys you a drink or presents you with a trivial gift of some sort, that is a sign he is interested in you.

* *Gaze*: when you are talking to a man in a meeting he will look at your eyes and forehead. In a social encounter he with look at your eyes and mouth. If he fancies you, he will subconsciously use a more intimate look in which his gaze focuses on your eyes but also takes in what I shall call your chest and/or what I shall call your lap. He will also be holding your gaze a smidgin longer than normal. Dilated pupils are further cues. When you fancy someone your pupils open wide, so if his pupils are large this is a clear sign he likes the look of you – either that or it's very dark.

* *Eyebrows flash*: a lightning-quick and subtle signal is when he opens his eyes wide and raises his eyebrows. Blink and you'll miss it.

* *Hands on hips*: this is the equivalent of one of those toads inflating his neck. It makes him look bigger. If his thumbs are in his belt and his legs are spread in the cowboy posture this is a frank courtship cluster, his thumbs pointing to, and accentuating, what I shall call his trouser region.

* *Crotch display*: if he spreads his legs it's rather like the market trader setting out his stall. I've seen a seated man exhibiting the crotch display slide his heels either side of the legs of the woman opposite. A very aggressive and frank sexual move. If this happens to you, you're definitely in business.

* *'Would you like to see my etchings?'*: he may be lacking in originality but not in clarity. Best of luck!

❁ *The first etchings were printed by Daniel Hopfer (c. 1470–1536).* ❁

How to
Pour Beer for a Gentleman

U nless you are a barmaid the chances are that whenever you pour beer for a gentleman you will be doing it from a bottle or can. The technique for dispensing beer through a little tap from a barrel or cask is similar to the bottle method, but serving chilled carbonated lagers and keg beers in a pub or rugby club requires a slightly different handling that I shan't go into here.

The first thing to remember is that beer drinkers, like art critics and jazz enthusiasts, are divided into a number of hard-boiled factions each of which disagrees with and hates the others. Your beardy real ale drinker will happily swallow a warm pint that's as flat as a mill pond and cloudy – with bits in, but will insist on half an hour's debate about its manufacture. While your lager man will demand a bright, clear icy cold drink with a good head on it – but not five inches of foam. Guinness fans, by contrast, are split into the bottle variety, who expect a room temperature drink with a brownish head of large bubbles that quickly dissipates, and the tap, keg and fizz-gizmo-can lot who want a cold drink with an inch of almost white 'cream' on top.

The method I've set out below is therefore a general technique that ought to help you do the job nicely for a range of beer-drinking types without making any of the basic mistakes, such as pouring ¾ pint of froth, or putting a cask-conditioned bottle beer into a very cold fridge.

INSTRUCTIONS

1   Open the can or bottle. *If it is cold it will be more lively* than a warm drink and will therefore require more careful handling. Real ale and live beer (see below) should be served at room temperature, not fridge-cold.

2   Anyway, hold the glass under the can or bottle and tilt its bottom up slightly. Touch the bottleneck or can to the lip of the glass and *slowly* elevate the can or bottle's bottom so that the liquid flows down the side of the glass rather than falling all the way to the foot. Doing it this way will prevent an excessive release of carbon dioxide bubbles, which will quickly fill the glass with froth. *Go slow.* This is the single most important beer-pouring rule.

3   If you are serving a pint in a pint glass, make sure you fill it right to the top so that the head, or meniscus if it's a stillish beer, sits above the rim. The only beer you don't have to do this with – and it's *the law* under the weights and measures act – is Guinness.

Being served short measures absolutely infuriates chaps in pubs and it's as well to bear this in mind even at home. You should always allow a lively beer to settle a bit and top it up to give a full pint. You will receive points for this. But be aware of regional discrepancies. Northern drinkers are used to a bit more head on their beer, while a fuller – flatter – pint is expected in the south.

A pint glass must either hold more than a pint, and have a line on the glass indicating the pint mark, or be a whole pint when full to the brim. Both kinds of glass carry a crown mark to show they are proper but we are on the cusp of European change in the pints department and the CE mark is superseding the crown: another bit of the kingdom going to the dogs.

4   Guinness and other stouts are not as hard to pour as people imagine. The stuff in the can sometimes comes with a plastic gadget in it that will make it foam for you as you open it. Bottle Guinness should be poured like any other bottle beer and will have a similar sort of head – much less dense. So don't worry that you've done something wrong. You haven't.

5   *Bottle-conditioned* beer requires a particular technique because it is still live and fermenting in the bottle – you'll see the yeast sediment in there. There are two schools of thought: the Drinkers and the Leavers. If serving a Leaver, you should go *even slower* than you were already to avoid shaking up the sediment as you

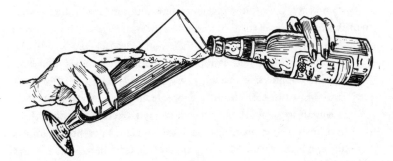

pour. And don't open a bottle that's just arrived from the super-market. Keep an eye open as you near the last quarter of the bottle and the moment you see the first grey whisp of sediment, stop pouring and discard the dregs. This yeasty sediment is actually quite harmless. So if you are serving a sediment Drinker, pour as usual but as you reach the last eighth of the bottle swirl the liquid gently to mix the sediment into the beer. Then gently pour the cloudy remains into the glass.

6   It's always best to wear a dirndl when serving beer to a gentleman.

❀ *1 imperial pint equals 1.20 US (wet) pints.* ❀

What to do with a Snoring Man

*J*ust imagine the picture: you lay aside *Pride and Prejudice* with a sympathetic sigh, switch out the light and start dozing off dreamily, thinking lovely thoughts. The next thing you know, you are brutally awakened by a spectacular noise like a gigantic walrus roaring through a didgeridoo into a tank full of blancmange. Yes, once again the man next to you is snoring for England (Wales, Scotland, etc.). Amazing how the hunky chap who once seemed so darkly handsome and mysterious can turn like Dr Jekyll into a snoring, belching, guffing ape creature who nightly tears the duvet off you and rolls himself up in it utterly oblivious.

You *must* act. The following are a few snoring causes, along with their remedies.

* *Booze*: everything relaxes including the throat muscles. Tell him that his floppiness is leaving you *unfulfilled*.
* *Smoking*: causes all kinds of problems such as super-mucus, inflamed naso-pharyngeal passages and Scratchy Throat. Get him to stop by explaining that smoking causes permanent impotence, which it can. Milk is a mucus-maker too, so watch out if he's a Horlicksaholic.

* *He's overweight*: fatty tissue around the neck can block his airway. Get him to cut down on the pizzas, curries and beer, and do more exercise.

* *Sleeping position*: when he sleeps on his back the root of his tongue is more likely to fall back and cover the airway (*see sleep apnoea* below). Try giving him more pillows to sleep on or get him to sleep on his side. Tennis balls sewn into his pyjamas was a remedy recommended by my milkman. It worked for him – apparently. At a push, you could try rolling him over, or calling his name and telling him to roll over. Works best with a non-blotto guy.

* *Allergies*: replace his feather pillows with something synthetic. Don't let him take antihistamines before he drops off. They can do more harm than good snorewise.

* *Sleep apnoea*: this is a serious – indeed life-threatening – condition in which the subject stops breathing for short periods. It also results in low-quality sleep, causing the poor fellow to walk round all day like a zombie. Get him down to the GP; it's treatable, in severe cases, by surgery.

One young man I used to know once told me that he snored so loudly he actually woke himself up. He cured it, he said, by going to sleep in the spare room. Our relationship foundered on such allegedly witty remarks. But the spare room is indeed an effective measure of last resort. Either him or you, it doesn't matter. So remember: laugh and the world laughs with you; snore and you sleep alone.

SOME OTHER TIME-TESTED REMEDIES.

1   Hit him.

2   Hit his pillow.

3   Earplugs (for *you* obviously).

4   Nasal strips and a variety of masks that are designed to keep the nose passages open. There is also some kind of dental appliance that is meant to pull his lower jaw and tongue forward so there's

more room at the back of the throat. These all sound a bit freaky to sleep next to though.

5   Go to bed first so that you are asleep by the time the snoring starts. (You're entering the desperate zone because this only works if his decibel level is low enough that it only bothers you while you're trying to drop off.)

6   Exercise all day so you are exhausted and impossible to wake. (You've clearly lost it.)

I can't promise success with any of the above, I'm afraid, but they are all worth a try even if the suspense ends up killing you, because it's such a relief when one night, after months of insomnia and recrimination, you sense triumph. For half an hour you wait with every nerve on the alert, but there comes no other sound save the chiming clock and the rustle of the ivy on the wall.

Hooray!

❀ *The biggest market for Horlicks is India.* ❀

Correct Toilet Seat Procedure in a Shared Dwelling Place

On the wonderful wooden trains of long ago there used to be a notice in the loo that said, in the terse prose of the time: 'Gentlemen lift the seat.' Was this a philosophical premise, a bald statement of fact or maybe a suggestion that any man who didn't was not a gentleman? What it really was of course was a forlorn request disguised as an imperative.

Although we are certainly glad when the gentleman does lift the seat, the main problem really comes, of course, when he doesn't put it back down again. If you live somewhere with a lot of men – or even just one man – the raised seat problem can move beyond the forlorn-request stage to become a daily botheration that may, with the cumulative power of water dripping on a grey stone, wear you down over months, years or even decades. I've never heard of anyone divorcing her husband just because of careless, or even willfully improper, toilet seat procedure but it wouldn't surprise me.

Let us examine the arguments. I am for the moment excluding the top – hole-lacking – seat from the discussion because things are quite complicated enough without that.

FUNCTION

* There is only one way that ladies can use the toilet and that is with the seat down. If you've ever wandered into a dark loo in a shared student flat in the middle of the night and sat down, forgetting to check first, then you will know just how startling it can be to find yourself suddenly with your knees against your chin, your lower legs sticking out horizontally in front of you, and the cold hand of the vitreous china against your bum.
* Men, on the other hand, have the luxury of choice. And since, most of the time, they can go standing up, it makes sense for them to lift the seat and replace it after use. Some of the time down will be right for them anyway (point 1).
* Note: for reasons best known to himself, the actor Kenneth Williams always insisted on sitting on the porcelain. Not surprisingly a seat one day fell against him, causing nasty scratches to his back. This only confirms, I think, that down is the sole reliable seat position.

STATISTICS

* Statistics show that women are more frequent users of the lavatory than are men, even once you allow for things like chaps availing themselves of the rose bushes, going behind fences or writing their names in the snow. The argument for down is, therefore, further inclined in our favour (point 2).

AESTHETICS

* A bit like opinions about *The Scream*, *The Rape of the Sabines* or something by Mark Rothko, the aesthetics of toilet seat position are what you might call a grey area, a sort of backwater of the art criticism racket. Who, after all, is to say whether up is more pleasing than down?

* Well, although the argument is one that is likely to end in fisticuffs, I think a very good case can be made for down being the natural, normal and most pleasing TSP (Toilet Seat Position), as well as the safest. There is a wholeness, an authority, a settled-British-horizontal-landscapeness to down, with something of Gainsborough about it. Up is much more angular, unhappy-diagonal-Cubist, with out-of-tune-Stravinsky musical overtones. It's Expressionist-Russian rather than British; less your John Constable, more your Wassily Kandinsky, and I don't know about you but I definitely don't want to sit on a Wassily Kandinsky thank you very much (point 3)

The final position is clear. Down is the proper default position for the toilet seat in a shared dwelling place, with up an acceptable temporary position only. So please: gentlemen lift the seat, but put it down again afterwards.

❋ *In August 2004* The Scream *was stolen from Oslo's Munch Museum.* ❋

How to
Descend a Staircase
in High Heels

There was this woman I used to know who wore high heels every day in the office. You could hear her coming down the corridor like a ticking bomb. She always looked perfect and you just knew she was wearing real stockings too. She was that kind of a woman.

It's true that high heels do something for a woman, causing the buttocks to tense, emphasising the calf muscles, adding height (always good) and making you walk in that quintessentially poised, feminine way, as if stepping along a ribbon with a book on your head.

But, *gawd*, they can be a nightmare to wear. Your centre of gravity is higher and you have to learn to balance with your bottom and boobs pushed out and your hips jiggling to compensate. Coming down a curly staircase in a ballgown and stilettos is an activity simply fraught with hazard. But here, along with some other high heel know-how, is the way to do it, so that next time you find yourself at the Palace with a prince on your arm you can come downstairs like Kim Novak in *Vertigo* instead of like Dandy Nichols in curlers.

Practise

It is logarithmically harder to walk in six-inch heels than it is in five-inch heels; a bit like stilts. Indeed, six-inch heels are for the experienced only, so start with a nice low heel, moving up in half-inch increments – it's not going to happen overnight. *Note*: heel height is the distance from floor to the sole of the shoe.

Buy good shoes that fit properly. Wedge heels are easier than stilettos and better for the lino, and strappy ones can feel more secure. To begin stand in front of a full-length mirror to get used to the feel, and examine your new posture, then walk a few steps towards the mirror and back again, building up slowly.

Take shorter steps than usual, coming down heel first in the usual way but with most of the weight on the ball of your foot. Stand erect, don't lean forwards. The reinforced heel will prevent you falling backwards. Before you go out wear your heels around the house for a while as you watch telly and go about your business. But look out for loose rugs and slippery parquet. Point your toes straight ahead, with each new step coming down directly in front of the last, as if you were walking a narrow plank. Once you can gracefully carry a tray of full wineglasses across a carpet like this you will know you have mastered the basics.

THE STAIRCASE

OK, so you can walk about. But now you are faced with the staircase, and all the eyes are on you. How are you going to handle it? Only the most brazen would slide down the banister. No, take hold of the rail, a man in a tux or, even better, both, and begin your descent. The technique is slightly different to walking on the floor, in that the whole foot should come down flat on the step instead of heel first. To add stability, turn your body – and feet, obviously, or you'll look like the India-rubber woman – so that you are coming down at a slight sideways angle to the stairs. Your feet should strike each step off the perpendicular. Not only is this the fitting way for a lady to descend the stairs, it reduces the possibility of her toppling forwards in a shower of pearls and tumbling down the stairs like Buster Keaton. Grip that banister but do it nicely. *Note*: If you're wearing a long gown, take pains not to tread on the hem or the gallery will echo to the sound of rending satin, and you might trip.

Don't walk on snow, mud, lawns, beaches or long gravel drives. You'll either sink like a candle holder into a birthday cake or just topple over in the old-fashioned way. Instead, do like the Bond-girls do and go barefoot, with your precious high heels cradled safely in your arms.

❋ *'Whoever invented high heels, women owe him a lot.' Marilyn Monroe.* ❋

How to

Get Out of a Car Without Flashing your Knickers

When you're a student and you find yourself with a curry in your arms being unceremoniously forced backwards out of a knackered old Volkswagen Beetle in jeans and a manky old Parka, it doesn't really matter. But when you emerge slinkily from a throbbing red Ferrari or a purring black Rolls Royce to the popping of flash bulbs you'd better do it right and look the part. The move should be smooth, practised, swift and elegant.

Here are the essentials, so that next time you get out of a car – as a passenger in a right-hand-drive vehicle – you will look more like the svelte Jennifer Lopez than the lumpen Tracey Tunstall.

CLOTHES

For a start off, you'd better wear the right knickers, just in case it all goes pear shaped. So not your favourite great big belly-hugging Grandma Moses pants in a tasteful greyish-white, nor the old faves with the holes, that you wear because they're nice 'n' comfy. These had better be pretty to look at.

While it's fine to wear a mini skirt, it's going to make the job that much trickier. So do yourself a favour and pull it down as far as you can before you open the door. If you try to leave the motor with the skirt snarled round your hips, I'm afraid it's not going to be pretty.

If your skirt or dress is longish and flowing, make sure your knees are covered before you turn (*see* below) so that your legs will pull the material after you in a controlled way, without it riding up or snagging your feet. And mind that gear stick.

THE BUSINESS

1   Once you are sartorially fixed up and ready to go, open the door as far as you can. Ideally a gentleman should do this for you from the outside. Don't stretch out all undignified into the street. Keep your body erect as far as possible.

2   Whatever you do from now on, imagine that your knees have been stuck together with a piece of tight elastic. The cardinal rule is to keep those knees touching whenever you possibly can. Place your left leg out and step on to the ground. The right leg should follow quickly, closely and smoothly.

3   Swivel your body towards the exit, keeping your knees together. Both feet should be firmly planted on the ground in front of you. Keep them still.

4   If you can support yourself on the hand of a gentleman outside the car as you exit, do so. Place your left hand on the seat beside

you and push down firmly. Rest your right hand on his and pull yourself gracefully up. He will take your weight and help you out. Don't loose hold and fall backwards smacking your head against the car in an unladylike way. If there is nobody to assist, place both hands either side of your bum and push up. It is more dignified to keep you hands low, rather than grab desperately at the door-frame. It should all look smooth and easy. Any strenuous grunting and wriggling is to be avoided.

5 Bob your head gracefully as you leave the car to avoid banging it painfully on the sharp surround.

6 At no time should you swear.

7 Stand effortlessly, making certain that you have a secure footing, and either allow someone else to shut the door or do it yourself –

nicely not like you're in a mood. It is only too easy, having left the car gracefully, to spoil it all by losing your balance and staggering about on your high heels with a desperate look on your face. Either that or bending an ankle agonisingly as you step out and going down like a felled antelope.

Work hard and do as the professionals do by practising in private before daring to perform your exit in public. Then if you do happen to flash your thigh and panties, you'll do it sexily so that you receive admiring wolf whistles, not flatulent raspberries, from the ugly scrum on the red carpet.

❀ *Aston Martin was founded in 1913 by Lionel Martin and Robert Bamford.* ❀

How to
Fart with Grace and Charm at the Ambassador's Do

Since Chaucer, people have been writing funny things about farts but the subject must surely have been amusing the masses long before *The Miller's Tale* (1386). I bet cavemen and -women without number sat round the fire farting like gooduns and roaring with laughter whenever somebody let one go.

Certainly the language of farting is centuries old. The word 'fart' comes from the Old English *feortan*, derived from the Old High German *ferzan*, and is related to the Old Norse *freta*, from the Germanic *fertan*. So now you know.

Letting one fly in public can be problematic in our modern – civilized – world. Loud traffic, music and general hubbub can all provide a useful cover if timing is nicely judged, but they are not infallible. Thinking himself adequately shielded by the climax of a boisterous Strauss march during a brass band concert in Orpington, my Uncle Bob told me he let off a sneaky one against the rough surface of his canvas chair but was caught out by the abrupt ending of the music. The mayor, I'm told, was visibly shaken by the undisguised ferocity of it in the sudden silence of the reverberant chamber.

At an ambassadorial function, things are trickier because you are more exposed; indeed, you have nowhere to hide. There is therefore a need for general caution, to avoid frightening the horses, and you wouldn't want to send a plate of those Italian chocolates flying with a mistimed venting. But get your timing right and things should be OK. Here are a few ideas.

* *The string quartet*: the cello's *con brio* passages are the ones to look out for.
* *The opportunist*: waiter noisily dropped a tray of wine glasses? Now's your chance.

* *The cigarette manoeuvre*: go on to the balcony to light a cigarette.
* *The dissembler*: just say, 'Good gracious, Mr Ambassador, your hinges need oiling.'
* *Trumpets and drums*: my friend Ingeborg (we used to call her 'ironing board') was once involved with the Nobel Prize ceremony. She suspected from the far-away look on their faces that many nervous recipients were timing their emissions to coincide with the trumpet fanfare. If you ever receive the Nobel Prize take a leaf from their book.

* *The applause ruse*: are they clapping a speech? What better coverage?
* *Brazen it out*: if push comes to shove, simply smile and *dare* anyone to challenge you.

❀ *Alfred Nobel invented dynamite in 1867: US patent 78,317.* ❀

How to
Invite a Gentleman to Tiffin

*T*he tiffin delivery system of Mumbai (Bombay) is so efficient that the dabbawalas – the largely illiterate men who deliver thousands of tiffins every day to hungry workers across the city – make only one mistake per million deliveries. 'Tiffin', of course, is an English term for a light meal eaten during the day that was enthusiastically adopted by the natives in the time of the British Raj. I think if I'd been invaded by bossy tiffin-supping colonists in pith helmets, my advice to them would have been: 'Piths off!'

The term (tiffin, not piths off!) crops up in Dickens and Thackeray but has now faded from use in Britain. Nevertheless, I think it's time for a revival. So if you'd like to know the proper way to invite a gentleman to tiffin, here it is.

INSTRUCTIONS

The world does not have a heart attack any more if a lady invites a gentleman round, nor does it insist that the door of her drawing room be kept open while he's there. But formality is still *the thing*. All formal invitations, whether engraved or written yourself with a quill pen, should be proffered with punctilious ceremoniosity. So you must use the third person. As the man said: good usage permits of no deviation from this form. You should expect to receive acceptances and regrets in the same dry distant arm's-length fashion. Whatever you do, don't just send a text saying: 'r u cumng 4 tiff'. It lacks grace.

Mrs Beeton, who knew all about this sort of thing, allows that the form of words in an invite may be varied – in proportion to the intimacy *or position* of the host and guest. Do not, whatever you do, get out of place in the pecking order. This is how it should look:

Miss Lady presents her compliments to Mr Gentleman,
and requests the honour [or *hopes to have the pleasure*] *of his*
company to tiffin on Tuesday, the 11th of February next.

CAREY STREET,

January 15th, 2020. RSVP

RSVP is a French politeness, standing for *Répondez, s'il vous plaît*. It means: 'Kindly let me know if you're coming and don't leave me hanging about like last time, wondering whether to get in extra Carlsberg Special Brew that afternoon or not.'

❀ *Isabella Beeton died in 1865, aged just 28.* ❀

How to
Organize a
Rip-Roaring Street Party

*H*ardly a day went by in the 50s and 60s without a street party of some kind or another taking place in neighbourhoods across the land. And what jolly occasions they were too, featuring rosy-cheeked children, dressed impeccably (like adults), sitting up straight and chuckling with fun as they listened to *Nellie The Elephant* and *The Bee Song* on a wind-up gramophone: boys in shirts, shorts and ties, girls in pink frocks, pigtails and pretty shoes. Mums sporting quilted house-coats and headscarves would pass round jelly, and that supernatural British version of ice cream, while Brylcreemed dads – smoking ciga-rettes for their throats' sake – leaned ladders against hot stink pipes to adjust the bunting, in tweed jackets with leather buttons.

I suppose the last street party bearing any resemblance to this idyll must have happened in the Queen's silver jubilee year of 1977. If you visited one today, you'd more likely find an ugly mob of surly children dressed in trainers, hoodies and shell suits, with iPods stuck in their ears, slouching over PSPs as a smattering of their single parents, rudely dressed (like children) in baseball caps and PE kit, sent foul-mouthed text messages to each other across an ill-kept stretch of disfigured tarmac to the sound of some screaming punk or heavy metal band.

Well, in case you'd like to conjure up the street parties of yesteryear, here are a few hints and tips.

Planning and organization
Start planning in spring with a few enthusiastic neighbours and agree a date early on. A Sunday in early September is good. Set a sensible schedule, say: cars away by 11am, lunch by 2pm, tea party at 5pm with children retiring at a sensible time and adults carousing into the early hours, as they clear up. Keep it simple and it should be a terrific day.

Involve everyone
Invite every household (and business) in the street, and consult them about the road closure. Apply three months in advance to your council's highways section for permission to close the road. If you live in Piccadilly, best forget it and just have a knees-up in St James's Park.

You'll get a more positive response by knocking on doors than you will with a note through the letterbox and you won't have to work round several grumpy old men. Your council may want to see evidence that you have consulted everyone so send written invitations nearer the time. Follow up with a reminder to people the day before, and ask them to move their cars in good time.

Involve people by asking them to contribute their special skills: Miss Smiley does the door-to-door invitations while Mrs Cook masterminds the food and Mr Jolly entertains the children during the lulls. Mr Sharpe can be in charge of discipline.

Safety
Most street parties should not need special insurance but your council may insist on it. However, it will come in at a manageable sum, usually between £50 and £100. Make sure that everyone agrees to be sensible and take responsibility for themselves.

Things to do
* If you are running the party, remain visibly in charge and all will go smoothly.
* Put up your bunting in good time to create a sense of expectation.
* Music really puts people in the mood and it's best if it's live. Most

parts of town have a few amateur musicians lurking. Not too loud though.

* Sit-down meals at fixed times lend the event a proper sense of occasion.
* Have a few well-run party games in the middle of the street but don't go on too long.
* If you have a fire-eater in the neighbourhood, you're well away.
* Work around uncooperative neighbours. Just throw a tarpaulin over them and bump their cars round the corner.

In church hall if wet.

❀ *In 1977 some 4,000 street parties were held in London.* ❀

How to
Pass Off a Shop-Bought Meal as Your Own

*F*anny Cradock was odd. I challenge anybody to refute that declaration. Although she was hailed as the first modern TV cook, her food suffered, I always felt, from the same problems as her face, that is to say, too much makeup. Fancy though her meals were made to appear on telly, with spun sugar, cream and exotic sauces, I understand she ate frugally at home, off a diet of baked beans, Bisto, gin, instant custard and suchlike. It was a case of what you saw was what you didn't get, or maybe what you got was what you didn't see.

This is the approach to take when passing off a shop-bought meal as homemade. And it is a useful skill to have up your sleeve, just like cardiopulmonary resuscitation. Let us assume that you have spoiled a meal to the point that it is beyond saving? If it *can* be saved *see* page 98: *How to rescue a meal that's gone wrong*. Your guests are due in half an hour and you are frantic. But fear not, by using a little imagination you can save the day. The tips set out here may be used with carefully bought meals or with take-aways. So wipe your tears – not on your apron, that would be unhygienic – and get to work. Remember: imagination is the key to success here.

INSTRUCTIONS

1   First, if you are panicking, stop.

2   Open the windows to get rid of the smoke.

3   Light a scented candle or joss stick to mask the odour of nuclear conflagration.

4   Remove all traces of the disaster meal (take burnt remnants outside to dustbin).

5   Scour the cupboards and freezer to find anything useable. Let's suppose you discover that you have little beyond a large bar of chocolate, hidden from your flatmates, some fresh herbs, a five-year-old frozen gateaux and a few vegetables.

6   Defrost the cake in the microwave.

7   While doing this, slowly fry an onion in butter. This smells delicious and is the first of your deceptions, since this onion will never be eaten. The purpose of this olfactory appetite-whetter is to seduce your guests' nostrils as they arrive.

8   Ring the *best* take-away place and order what you please. OK, it's expensive and you don't get that thrill of culinary accomplishment, but beggars can't be choosers.

9   When it arrives *disguise it*:

   * *Remove all packaging and transfer to nice serving dishes.* Nobody will be fooled if you spoon it out of a foil carton.

   * *Always add something of your own*, eg cherry tomatoes, cheese, fresh mushrooms and olives to the top of a pizza; fresh cream and a yoghurt, cucumber and mint side dish to a curry; and longitudinally sliced spring onions to a Chinese meal.

   * *Herbs*: whatever you are serving, strew plenty of fresh herbs all over the place.

   * *Curries*: try cooking your own rice to go with a curry and serve it all sizzling from nice hot dishes.

* *A crumbled Flake* added to a chocolate pudding that comes in the form of a powder out of a packet will turn it into a delicacy.
* *Black Forest gateau*: disguise the factory processes by grating plenty of chocolate all over it, including on the plate. Very deceptive, that is.

10 Once your guests arrive, keep away from that microwave at all costs. Those pings tell tales.

❀ *The Black Forest is a wooded mountain range in Baden-Württemberg.* ❀

How to
Rescue a Meal That's Gone Wrong

*D*o you remember when we all had much more time and much less stuff; when plumbers earned *less* than teachers and hardly any of us had second homes; when nobody worked such stupid hours and we all had time to cook an evening meal? You don't? Well I'm not making it up – there really was such a time.

Of course the advantages of *not* cooking dinner and getting a take-away are many, and the main one is that a take-away is unlikely to go wrong. The trouble with home-made is that, as often as not, what you hoped would be the perfect chocolate soufflé comes out of the oven all sunken and wretched. With this in mind I have prepared a few ideas for when it all goes wrong and you've got guests round. They cover generalized problems, but are applicable in particular situations. With any luck, they should save your bacon.

CULINARY FIRST AID
* *Too lumpy*: if making custard, gravy or sauce, keep a whisk to hand to get rid of lumps. Still lumpy? Strain through a sieve.
* *Too runny*: mix cornflour and water in a small cup and add to liquid a little at a time, stirring constantly. Not too fast, if the liquid is hot, because it will *suddenly* thicken, leaving you with a

saucepan of 'concrete' hanging from your wooden spoon. And be patient – don't add too much cornflour or you'll end up serving your gravy in *slices*.

* *Too salty*: if it's soup or gravy, add more water. This will put you in the too-runny scenario so use the too-runny remedy. If it then gets too lumpy do the too-lumpy business. Don't go on all night like this or you'll have hundreds of gallons of unwanted sauce.

* *Burnt*: if it's a saucepan do not stir, but remove at once from the heat. You may be able to rescue the top few inches (but *taste* it. There's nothing more penetrating than the flavour of burnt polytetrafluoroethylene (Teflon). In any case, it's wise to turn the mess into a curry to hide the smack of carbonized aluminium.

* *Too spicy*: boil up vegetables with no salt or flavouring and add this pulp to dilute the tang. A libation containing alcohol (vodka) or fat (milk) will dampen the ferocious chemical firestorm in the mouth. But don't serve water, which exacerbates the problem.

* *Overcooked meat or pie gone hard*: make a thinish sauce and simply saturate the hardened foodstuff to disguise the problem. Hardened pastry is particularly amenable to the absorption process. Overcooked cakes, buns and biscuits can be turned into a trifle base if soaked in a fruity sauce or jelly.

❀ *Clean burnt pans by boiling in a sodium bicarbonate and water solution.* ❀

How to
Write the Perfect Thank-You Letter

When I was a girl my mum would stand over me with a switch after some blasted holiday or other as I painfully crafted my thank-you letters to aunts, grandmas, godfathers and benefactors of every kind. Christmases and birthdays were vitiated by the thought of these wretched dispatches and I never really knew what to say anyway, especially if I wasn't actually grateful for the present. It's hard to write a thank-you for something insultingly cheap and unimaginatively inappropriate without the taint of intellectual dishonesty leaking into your soul. Often I felt like saying:

> Dear Auntie Lettice: thank you so much for the Fuzzy Felt farm (with the 'Reduced!' price tag still on it) which might have been appropriate 10 years ago when I was 7. What's your problem lady? Has the old brain finally gone completely soft or something? Wake up and smell the roses, and at least *pretend* to try – you silly old cow!

But I never did.

Of course it's not just gifts; there are all kinds of things to acknowledge, such as somebody's attendance at a wedding, or their looking after your dog when on holiday (when *you* were on holiday, not the dog). There are formal letters for buttering up clients who have put business your way and polite notes to your prison visitor thanking her for the cake with the file in it (*see* page 248).

So here are a few hints and tips to reduce the agony.

* Most of the stuff that comes through my letterbox goes straight in the bin so it's lovely to see a real letter on the mat. Your having written at all will nowadays surprise and delight the recipient of your letter, especially if she is older than 40; and you'll probably find your teenage friends appreciate it too. So don't imagine your efforts will go unnoticed.
* It goes without saying that emails and texts don't count. If it goes without saying, why did I say it? Clearly it doesn't go without saying.
* Use a pen rather than type it out; it adds that personal touch. No need to write on vellum with a quill though, or seal it with wax.
* Always send your letter promptly. A late thank-you somehow draws attention to your failure to say thank you earlier. Strange but true.
* If it's a present you're thanking them for, make sure you know what it was. There's nothing more deflating to a proud giver than

a vague thank-you which makes it clear that the sender hasn't got the first idea what she got. And don't print out a generic letter and send it to everyone, with just their name written in at the top in crayon. It's always obvious, especially if givers compare notes. And you wouldn't want to appear petit bourgeois would you.

* Say something particular about the gift: how useful, original or, sweet-smelling it is. Tell them it is an article you have wanted for ages but would never have thought to buy for yourself. But be sensible: it's unconvincing to describe a book token as original or just what I've always wanted'.

* If you don't have much to say, use a postcard – this saves you from writing in huge characters like Helen Keller, or with miles of space between the lines, and is a welcome antidote to the composition of great long sentences full of padding, pleonasm, unnecessary verbiage, gassy circumlocution, excessive prolixity, wordiness, long-winded loquacity, sesquipedalian verbosity, and periphrastic grandiloquence. Nobody's fooled by that.

❀ *Спасибо is Russian for 'thank you'.* ❀

IV

How to be Completely Gorgeous

Glamour, makeup and wardrobe tips for the busy girl

I have flabby thighs, but fortunately my stomach covers them.

JOAN RIVERS

17 Uses for a Spare Fishnet Stocking

*H*ow many times have you been woken by the click of your bedroom door closing the morning after the night before only to find you're a fishnet stocking short? That was a rhetorical question; please don't send me autobiographical postcards. Unless you are a one-legged lady, there isn't a lot of use for a single stocking. Or so you'd think. But think again, because here are a few ideas.

1   *Used carrier bag holder*: cut a small toe hole and stuff your used shopping bags in the top of the leg. When you need a bag for drowning some kittens or something, just pull one from the toe.

2   *Salad spinner*: this works a treat. Carefully drop your lettuce, radish and wet legumes into the toe and go outside. Spin the stocking round your head like a sling, holding the fat end. But don't let it go or one of your neighbours is going to get the surprise of his life.

3   *Hammock for soft toy in car window*: if you are sad enough to want one of these, then get yourself some of those window sucker things and you're away.

4   *Drain cover*: tired of bits and pieces going down the sink? Scrunch stocking, stuff into drain and *hey presto!* it's an instant straining device.

5   *Flour sieve*: measure the flour, stand on a chair and sieve as normal.

6   *Tennis ball holder*: what could be simpler?

7   *Hairnet*: they may be a bit out of fashion but you could start a new trend – the Ena Sharples *de nos jours*. Use the middle of the stocking and sew closed.

8   *Dog ball sling*: drop in a tennis ball and tie off directly above the ball. Swing it round your head and release across the park like the Hale–Bopp comet. Rover will retrieve it for you.

9   *Chip shop-style interior décor*: cut down side of stocking, pin out
     flat on wall and decorate with lobsterpot, crab, starfish, dried
     bladder wrack and glass buoy. True 70s chic. Lovely!

10   *Claustrophobic bank robber's face mask*: for the more neurotic rap-
     scallion.

11   *Smalls bag*: pop your pants, socks etc into the stocking and tie
     loosely then wash as usual. And *bingo!* no more lost sock misery.

12   *Plant support*: stretch the stocking leg over a wigwam of three
     canes in a flowerpot. Black-eyed Susans and morning glory seeds
     will gallop away.

13   *Sausage dog draft excluder*: pack the stocking with old rags and a
     heavy chain. Lay against the door (not *you*, the *stocking*) to stop
     the wind whistling under like a knife. (*See* page 52 for more on
     this subject.)

14   *Onion and ham nets*: hang onions, salamis and ham joints from the
     beams of your kitchen ceiling. Dead rustic.

15   *Butterfly net*: straighten out a wire coat hanger and thread through
     top of close-weave fishnet stocking. Bend hanger into rough

circle, twist wire ends together and poke into cane handle. Tie off and cut surplus netting.

16 *Magical bubble wand*: dip your butterfly net in a solution of washing-up liquid and water, and wave it around. *Oooh.*

17 *Animal feeder*: fill stocking with dandelion leaves and hang in corner of bunny cage.

18 *Bird feeder*: cram stocking with stale bread and bacon scraps and hang out beside your tit box.

And if you locate the other stocking down the back of the sofa after doing any of the above, don't blame me.

❋ *Fishing nets are made of synthetic polyamides.* ❋

How to
Buy the Right Size Bra

*H*hen I was chatting to the Queen recently I told her about the problem her female subjects sometimes have in getting hold of a bra that fits properly. You know: one that doesn't drive you mad by digging in like an elastic band round a raw sausage and extruding great squashy pads of fat. But it was no use; she couldn't hear me up on that balcony.

Despite her wry comment that, 'I have to be seen to be believed,' the Queen actually gets the best advice going when it comes to bra-land. I know this because in 1960, while she was granting Somalia its independence, she bestowed on Rigby & Peller – the famous Knightsbridge bra and pants firm – the Royal Warrant of Appointment, making them her official 'Corsetieres', and augmenting her own role as the country's titular head.

Sizing
Rigby & Peller say that some 80% of the women who come to them for an expert fitting are wearing bras that don't fit, which *I* could have told

them. You should see my red one with the raggedy straps: it's like being in a straitjacket. They recommend getting the thing properly fitted, and they also believe that a tape measure leaves a great deal to be desired when calculating bra size. Because so much hangs on the measurements and because we are all different – with a limitless diversity of body shapes – a tape measure can only be a crude guide.

It cannot be overstated that having your bra professionally fitted is by far the best way to do it. Women change shape and size over time, sometimes dramatically, so you should have a proper fitting regularly. Try on a range of styles from different brands: you'll find that some cuts will fit you better than others.

Working out what fits your bits

1   To make life difficult, there is no such thing as a definitive bra size. The size varies along with the style and fabric.

2   To put on a new bra, bend over and lower your boobs into the cups. Then stand up and wriggle about a bit in the old fashioned way, tucking in anything that's still hanging out.

3   Fasten the bra on the loosest hooks to start with – so long as the band is snug. It will loosen up with wearing, washing and wriggling. As it does so you can go tighter. If you have a plump back, three hooks are better than two.

4   Bras should be *hand washed*. Never tumble dry or hang on a radiator.

5   The band should lie snugly against the narrowest part of your back, in the middle, and level with the bra front. If the fit is correct you should be able to run your finger along the inside without having to saw it off to get it out again.

6   Try on your bra under a tight fitting top. You should look smooth and curvy. If you look like a bag of jackfruit, something's wrong.

7   Underwires should curve comfortably around your breasts. They should never cut in. To test whether it is doing its job properly, put the bra on and push against the wire. If it yields softly, it is resting on your breast, so try a larger cup size. If it feels hard, it is

lying against the chest wall, which is where you want it.

8   Move around in your new bra and lift your arms over your head. It shouldn't ride up, spill anything out, stop providing support or get all out of whack.

9   Common problems include the 'bulging tyre' effect that comes from too tight a band, and the 'hot cross bun' effect that comes from too small a cup.

10   If your boobs are spilling out the front, or your silhouette is lumpen, or you're falling out of the bottom of an underwire, try a bra with a smaller back and larger cups.

11   If the bra is loose round the edges try a smaller cup size.

12   If the band is riding up your back or if your straps are cutting in, try a smaller back size.

13   If the underwire is digging in below your armpit, try a bigger cup size.

14   If you have heavy boobs, non-stretch straps will provide a more dependable hold.

15   If your size goes up and down (common), get a bra with some stretch in it. If you have large fluctuations, get yourself some bras of different sizes.

16   Try a variety of bras for miscellaneous outfits and occasions: seamless, strapless, sports …

Finally, please remember that these are only tips and guidelines. The main point to keep in mind is that DIY in this department is unlikely to work for you. In fact you will probably make a complete boob of things. So fling away that tape measure and go and get a proper fitting from the professionals. You'll be glad you did.

❀ *Mae West spent 2 hours a day rubbing cold cream into her breasts.* ❀

How to
Do the Pencil Test

*U*ntil his retirement, my Uncle Bob was a salesman for a stationery company near Croydon. In his spare time he was also an expert snooker player, winning numerous trophies. When I was a teenager he used to take me along to pubs and snooker halls around the country to help him carry his cues, and it was during a tournament-lull in the village hall of Ryme Intrinseca in Dorset that he first introduced me to the history of the pencil. I remember him telling me that the earliest pencils were produced in Keswick round about 1558, but that it was the Italians who developed the wooden 'holder'.

Uncle Bob also introduced me to the pencil test. He told me that his second wife had been a martyr to it and that she used to stand for hours in front of her bedroom mirror, appraising her performance over and over and over. If you haven't heard about – or tried – the pencil test here is your chance to try it. It's a simple test designed to discover the condition and pertness of the female bust, and you can do it on, and for, yourself at a moment's notice.

REQUIRED
A pencil. The best pencils for the purpose are of smooth uncoated wood. Painted pencils have a greater predisposition to 'cling', thus skewing results.

INSTRUCTIONS
1   Go upstairs (if you have an upstairs) and make sure you will not be disturbed.
2   Take your things off and stand in front of a full-length mirror.
3   Place a wooden pencil horizontally under your breast of preference at its junction with the chest.
4   Stand still.

RESULTS ANALYSIS

A correctly positioned pencil that nonetheless falls is an indicator of top quality upwardly-pointing glands. Either the bra-wearing stage has not yet been reached (you must be young), or you are in extra fine fettle pertness-wise. If the pencil is held in place by the weight of the breast and does not fall (no jiggling allowed), then you have failed the test. However: this *should not* be seen as a critique of physique – possibly quite the reverse. Jayne Mansfield was a pencil test-failer of the first water if ever I saw one and she was a centrefold girl. Nonetheless, it is important to note that if the pencil can be removed only by pulling with both hands and rolling about on the floor then a really good uplifting bra is in order, and should be *on* order.

THE VERTICAL OR MAE WEST TEST

This one is for the ambitious.

Put on your most alluring bra and insert a pencil vertically into the cleavage. If it is held without falling, the cleavage is perfect.

❀ *The world's biggest pencil, on show in Malaysia, is 65ft long.* ❀

How to
Choose the Most Flattering Colours for your Face

Choosing the best colours for your skin, hair and eyes is, in practice, more of an art than a science – which doesn't mean there *isn't* some science in there. And it's an art that most people can master without training. But even when you know the colours that suit your hair and complexion it's still easy to make mistakes. You must have tried on a thing in the shop that looked great on the hanger only to tear it off in disgust once you saw what it did to your face. A good test is to stand in front of the mirror in bright daylight and hold the garment under your chin. If the colour suits you, you'll notice that:

* Your eyes will 'come alive': the colour being brought out
* Your skin will look better, younger and smoother
* Your face will seem to be lit by a professional
* You will look more attractive and interesting
* People will smile at you more

It's rather like the right frame on a painting – complementing it without overpowering it. The best frame can make a dull painting look beautiful. The wrong frame can simply swamp a good one.

If a colour is not for you, you may notice that:

* Your skin looks tonally uneven and a bit funny
* The garment shows up more than you do, like the frame example above
* Weirdly dark or coloured shadows contaminate your chin and neck
* You look just like Vincent Price in *House of Wax* (1953)

There are some pretty reliable rules of thumb for choosing the right colours and you probably have a few of your own that you stick to. For example, blue eyes and blonde hair almost always look especially pretty with blue, while brown, beige and white are often a good bet for brunettes. If you have ginger or red hair you probably know that green is a fantastically flattering colour for you. Never wrong. Colour temperature is important too though. Warm blues might be preferable to cold; cool reds more fetching than screaming pillar box vermilion.

You'll get compliments on your appearance when you are wearing an especially flattering colour. So whenever this happens make a note of the hue and start putting together a palette for your wardrobe that really works *for you*.

❀ *Lipstick is the most popular colour cosmetic.* ❀

How to

Give Yourself
a French Manicure

*T*he observation that a man's index finger is generally shorter than his ring finger, and that the reverse is true for a woman, was first recorded in the nineteenth century. Recent research has also suggested that finger ratio can be an indicator of aggression. The bigger the gap between a short index and a long ring finger – the more aggressive (*read* masculine). And it is certainly true that short stubby fingers covered in oil and holding a spanner look masculine, and long, slim well-manicured ones appear feminine.

The instructions on this page will tell you how to achieve the acme of elegant home manicure, and long-looking fingers, without having to take out a mortgage at the salon – just the cost of your nail varnish.

Women have been doing their nails for at least 5,000 years according to something I read somewhere, but the origin of the 'French manicure' is a bit hazy. 'French' is one of those appellations beloved of advertisers and marketing people because it gives a flavour of exotic chic to everything from kissing to knickers. No surprises then that the cosmetics company Orly first registered the trademark 'Original French Manicure' for a home manicure kit in 1978, and that the 'Frenchie' is one of the most asked for manicures in the salons of today.

The thing that sets the French manicure apart is the milky white tip to the nail, which, in combination with the characteristic 'nude' pink bit, emphasizes its length.

To complete your own perfect French manicure, just follow the steps below. But make sure your nails are in a decent state before you start. Be honest, if you are an incorrigible nail-biter you might do best investigating the fakery at the salon. And if you are a harpist or in the potting shed all day then long nails are just a pest; better read another page.

Whatever you do, please *practise* your Frenchie before going out on a date with a new gentleman. You don't want to raise your glass with fingers that look as if Jackson Pollock's been painting them.

REQUIRED

* *White nail varnish*
* *Clear or 'nude' nail varnish*
* *An orange-stick*
* *Nail scissors (or clippers)*
* *A nail file and fine emery board*
* *Self-adhesive stationer's hole reinforcers*

INSTRUCTIONS

1   Before you start painting your nails, remove any old nail varnish, using ordinary nail varnish remover and a cotton wool ball.

2   Wash your hands and soak your fingers in a bowl of warm water for a while to allow the skin and nails to soften up a little (if they prune you've gone too far), then give them a thorough dry.

3   Using an orange-stick, or something else designed for the purpose, gently push back the cuticles so they are neatly in line.

4   Carefully trim and shape your nails with scissors, clippers, nail file and fine emery board. Then give them a quick rinse and dry.

5   Now for the tricky bit. Paint the tip of each nail with white nail varnish. You need a confident and purposeful movement from a steady hand. It can be tricky but here's a brilliant dodge: peel off one of your hole reinforcers and tear it in half. Stick this to the end of your nail such that it provides a mathematically perfect radius guide to the curve. Paint the white in the little gap at the end of the nail and then wave your hand around and blow on it a bit in the usual way until the varnish becomes tacky. Depending on the varnish's opacity, you may need another coat but let the first dry or you'll be in a right old mess. Carefully peel off the sticker and *hey presto!* a nice crisp edge.

6   Once all your white tips are done, paint the whole nail with a clear or translucent pale-pink 'nude' colour. Don't do it all splodgy – about three strokes is all you need. The first straight down the middle, the next two down the sides. Then leave well alone. The brushwork will look a bit Impressionist for a while but it gradually blears into a smooth finish. You may find you need a couple of coats but don't keep trying to fiddle with it; you'll ruin it and have to start all over again. It's usually now that a man will wander in asking you to hold a wet fishing net or carboniferous piece of exhaust pipe. Don't. Neither should you be tempted to start scrubbing the doorstep or cleaning the fluff sausages from under your bed. Watch a bit of mindless telly or something instead and wait till the varnish is good and dry.

Once everything's hardened, apply a clear final coat to protect your glamorous French manicure. You can improve its durability by painting on a new topcoat each night. You can't keep this up for ever though or you'll have horrible scabrous nails an inch thick.

❀ *Fingernails are made of a tough protein called keratin.* ❀

Home hairdos I
The Plait Ordinaire

*D*o you remember Mr Teazy Weazy, who went like a withering flame through the groovy hairstyles of the fashion gadabouts of 60s London? By the end of it all he must have been completely and utterly lacquered. I recall a moody shot of Twiggy, from that time, with an enormous great plait over her shoulder, which goes to show that the plait has never really gone out of style. There's a man near me – even today – who wears plaits with pride. I'm not convinced they go with his donkey jacket, but there, if it was good enough for Cleopatra it should be good enough for anyone.

In case you've never plaited your own hair, here's a guide. It's easiest to get the hang of this by trying it out on someone else first.

REQUIRED

* *Ouchless hair elastics*
* *Hair brush*
* *A hair clip to secure layers and stray strands (a bulldog clip will do in an emergency)*

INSTRUCTIONS

Once you get a rhythm going, the plait ordinaire is easy. Your hair should be fairly long (or what's to plait?), and dry.

1   Brush your hair to remove tangles. Takes about three hours.
2   Sweep it back into the nape and divide into three equal clumps (Fig. A).
3   Take two clumps in your left hand (separated by a finger), and the third in your right. Bring your right hand over the top of the middle bunch and pass the right hand clump to your left hand, while passing the middle clump to your right hand. (Does that even begin to make sense?) You should now have two bunches in your left hand again, only they're different bunches than when you started (Fig. B).

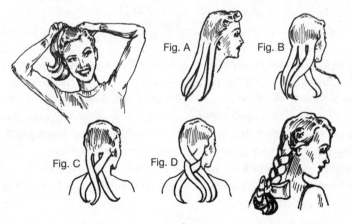

Fig. A   Fig. B

Fig. C   Fig. D

4   Cross the outside clump in your left hand over the new middle clump. You can use your right hand to grab this and bring it over, leaving two bunches in your right hand (Fig. C). (Get the idea?)

5   Pass the outside right bunch, over the middle.

6   You should now be looking at something resembling a plait. If you are looking at what looks like an explosion in a horsehair sofa factory, something's gone wrong. Anyway, let's presume you're doing OK. Keep crossing right over centre and then left over centre (Fig. D). This is the key to understanding the plait.

7   When you run out of hair, tie it off or secure with an elastic: a nice one, not one of those worm-coloured things the postman dropped on the path. Or dip it in tar like the jolly sailors of yesteryear.

The plait ordinaire is good for creating curls if you sleep with the plaits in.

❀ *Twiggy's mum worked in Woolworths.* ❀

Home hairdos II
The Plait Français

*B*odybuilding competitions for women began (of course) in the USA with such galas as the *Miss Physique* show, which looked to me like an old-fashioned bikini contest with added protein. But as the years rolled on, the iron was increasingly pumped by bodybuilding women till their biceps sprang out like Cornish pasties, their tummies rippled and some of them became hard to tell from Arnold Schwarzenegger before he became an intellectual and went into politics.

The reason I mention this is that the plait Français (sometimes known as the French braid) requires the elevation of your arms for absolutely ages and is utterly exhausting. All the blood flows out of your hands and the limbs begin to ache wearily; after a bit they start to wave around of their own accord like reeds in a pond, and finally they wither and drop, numb and lifeless, often falling heavily on your

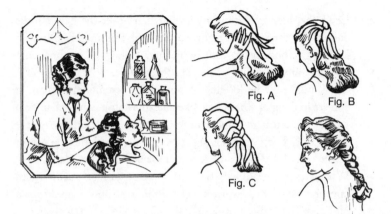

Fig. A

Fig. B

Fig. C

head and knocking your glasses off. But are you going to be so easily put off, or are you ready to join the ranks of bionic women, Miss Physique and the steely plaiters of purpose, and put your hair up in the plait Français? Oh good, that's what I hoped you'd say.

The main difference between the plait ordinaire (*see* page 115) and the plait Français is that, rather than just three strands of hair, more hair is introduced to the plait as you proceed. If you are doing it on yourself, remember that stamina is required.

INSTRUCTIONS

1   Separate the front part of your hair (including the sides) from the hair at the rear, pull the separated hair back to the crown and divide it into three equal clumps (Fig. A).

2   To start, do a quick left-over-centre, right-over-centre (as in the plait ordinaire). Don't bother being neat when you are learning (Fig. B). Most early efforts look like the work of one of those blind basket weavers the first time they try it. Once you're into your stride, you can begin to concentrate on maintaining tension and clump size, and things will begin to tidy themselves up a bit.

3   As you continue, add extra hair taken *from directly underneath each new section* that is about to be crossed over. Pick up the same amount

each time. Use your little finger to separate the clumps. This will let you hold the main hair firmly while you pick up the new hair. Your plait will follow the curve of the head as you go (Fig. C).

4   Keep on until you reach the nape and you've used up all the hair.
5   Finish with a plait ordinaire and secure with an elastic.

❁ *The main component of hair is keratin, just like fingernails.* ❁

Home hairdos III
How to Put Your Hair in a Bun

When I was young and foolish I used to think that ladies who wore their hair in a bun had to be at least 60 and possibly German. Maybe it was something to do with the word 'bun': sort of auntyish and brown, redolent of knitting needles, tweed skirts, and long grey Sunday afternoons destitute of interest, activity or anything except the perfume of shooting sticks, bluestockings, parched conservatories, worsted underwear, Murray Mints, dripping brogues, the *Times* crossword and Haliborange. It seemed to me the look to avoid.

Then one day as I was shopping in Mayfair I saw a tall gazelle-like young woman slinking along Bond Street in a most alluring way that I kind of wanted to emulate. She had – I found it hard to credit – her hair in a bun. As I watched her disappear up Bruton Place she withdrew from her tress a long pin, and shook down the hair all over her shoulders, like Sophia Loren in some film or other. *Aha*, I thought, *buns can be cool*.

If you'd like to try it, here are the instructions. You'll be really pleased to learn that you don't need to be neat when you're making a bun. A sort of wanton messed-up look is much better. Your hair, though, must be longer than shoulder-length.

INSTRUCTIONS

1   Finger-rake your hair back into a ponytail at the nape of your neck. This will give you a reckless, sexy and casual girl-about-town look. If you're after that prim-librarian-who-nevertheless-

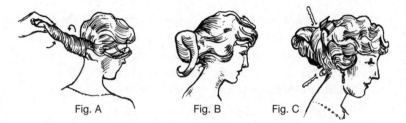

Fig. A   Fig. B   Fig. C

goes-wild-after-hours look then brush, for a neater effect. Secure with an elastic.

2   Twist the tail until the hair begins to bind and stiffen, recoiling on itself (Fig. A).

3   You can encourage a messy finish now if you pull a few short strands from near the ends of the ponytail.

4   Wrap the tail around on itself in the nape to make the bun (Fig. B).

5   Poke the end under the original covered band and then fix with a hairpin or grip. Don't use a clothes peg; it looks bad (Fig. C).

You can vary the look, and still turn heads, by sweeping the hair up into a bun at the rear from a low side parting or making a bun of just the crown of your hair and leaving the rest dangling seductively.

❀ *The Chelsea bun was created in the 18th century at the Chelsea Bun House.* ❀

The Imelda Marcos Guide to Shoes

*D*uring the 1992 Republican National Convention a man called Pat Robertson treated everyone to the benefit of his intellectual thoughtfulness. 'The feminist agenda,' he announced, 'encourages women to leave their husbands, kill their children, practise witchcraft, destroy capitalism and become lesbians.' Some felt he was going a bit far, and in 2006, in a defiant bid to show Mr Robertson what feminists are really like, the 77-year-old Imelda Marcos – former first lady of the Philippines – launched a range of jewellery, bags and trainers, which she selflessly christened the Imelda Collection. The Imelda Collection's very pink and possibly not-all-that-feminist website says: 'It is from the detritus of her colourful life, from the flotsam and jetsam of her own dramas, that Imelda makes jewellery.' Oh, yuck me sideways! Aren't people funny?

Anyway, to get back to the real world for a moment, here's a guide to shoes that Imelda would have killed for if she'd known about it before the arrival of the bunion years. See what you reckon.

Top tips

* Go shopping for shoes at the end of the day, when your feet are slightly larger. Otherwise your new shoes will only fit you in the morning.

* Try on both shoes if your feet are different sizes. (Common sense, surely.)

* According to Margaret Halsey: 'Englishwomen's shoes look as if they had been made by someone who had often heard shoes described, but had never seen any.' This may no longer be strictly true, but choose with care nonetheless.

* Have your feet properly measured once a year. That's not your boyfriend and you rolling around giggling with a ruler after a couple of Camparis.

* Wear tights when buying shoes that you will be wearing with tights. You wouldn't think it would make a difference but it does.

* For leather shoes, it's best to polish them while they are still soft and warm from wearing.

* If your shoes get wet, do not dry them over heat; they go really hard. Allow them to dry slowly, and stuff some newspaper inside to prevent shrinkage.

* Rotate your shoes. Not while you're walking, of course. I mean don't wear the same pair two days in succession.

* Keep your footwear sweet-smelling by putting orange peel inside them overnight. Or you can drip some lavender or lemongrass oil on a tissue and leave it in the shoes overnight.

* To freshen up old suede shoes, steam them over the kettle. Don't cook your hand.
* Keep unworn boots stuffed with newspaper. Unworn shoes benefit from a shoe tree.
* After a short walk on salted pavements in the winter your leather shoes can be spotted and stained. Mix 1tbsp vinegar with a cup of water and just wipe the marks off.
* Canvas shoes come up an absolute treat with the application of some carpet shampoo.
* If you think, like Fats Waller, that your feet's too big, try wearing high heels with chunky wedges. Pointy toes make your feet look longer, and feet in light shoes look bigger than in dark – so avoid. Detailing and flounces will make your feet more petite, so get out your feathers, your patent leathers, your beads and buckles and bows!

❀ *'Imelda' comes from the German words for 'entire' and 'battle'.* ❀

How to
Pluck Your Eyebrows

*A*s Ariel says in *The Tempest*: 'Where the bee plucks, there pluck I,' and who can blame him? There's something singularly architectural about a plucked eyebrow, that neither mascara nor subcutaneous botox can match. A really artistic pluck will draw attention to your eyes, just like a good picture frame, emphasizing and 'enlarging' the peepers and delineating the bone structure of your brow line. Heavy-duty plucking will be required to subjugate a vigorous brow-bush or divide a 'monobrow'. But while a touch of elegance or neatness is fine, don't go mad. The biggest mistake is to pluck to near baldness or to leave two insectoid 'antennae' over your minces. Eyebrows can take months to re-grow so go careful; leave more than a paltry scribble there on the outcrop. Here's the way the experts do it.

REQUIRED

* *Eyebrow pencil*
* *Proper angled eyebrow tweezers*

INSTRUCTIONS

1   You need good lighting. Full sun is best so sit near a window. Don't sit one inch from the mirror all the time. Lean back every now and again to have a look at your whole face and the general effect.

2   Wash your eyebrows with soap. This will make them thicker and easier to grasp.

3   Plan. Decide the shape you want and draw a guideline on your eyebrows, using an eyebrow pencil. The eyebrow should start at a point in line with the inner corner of your eye. Good rules of thumb are to make them thicker in the middle, and taper them in an elegant swoop to a point on the outside edge. Pluck a smooth, attractive arch, the highest point of which you can estimate by visualizing a line running from the corner of your nose at its junction with your cheek, through the centre of your pupil. Your brows will look most attractive if they extend a little beyond the corner of each eye. The space in between should be not less than an eye's width. Have a look at the models in your favourite magazine and copy theirs.

4   Use a pair of proper eyebrow tweezers. Doing it with pliers is bound to end in tears, and pluck hairs from *below* your brow, not from above.

5   Pull the skin tight at the temple and begin plucking in the middle of the eyebrow. Move towards the outer end, plucking only one hair at a time. Return to the middle and pluck towards the nose. Do a little bit of each eyebrow at a time. That way you'll get a balanced appearance instead of one big fat one and one skinny little one.

6   Finally rub your newly nudified brows with some cotton wool dipped in an astringent such as witch hazel.

❀ *The oldest known tweezers date from the 3rd millennium* BCE. ❀

A Quick Guide to Proper Deportment

When he was a little boy, my friend Antonio was made to eat spaghetti while balancing the *Dizionario Enciclopedico Italiano* on his head. Now he has beautiful manners, deports himself with élan and hardly ever pinches girls' bottoms.

In years gone by, deportment was a big thing in Britain too, especially for young ladies – a whole industry revolved around it and you wouldn't be seen dead in the street without pearls. This was the time when Swiss finishing schools and charm establishments for Chelsea girls (SW3 not NY) would groom debutantes-to-be in the niceties of polite manners, etiquette and posture, when elocution lessons were de rigueur for those unlucky enough to have been born common, but who wished to get on. In the glittering drawing rooms of Belgravia our own version of the Italian encyclopaedia trick was to get a young lady, coifed and gowned, to promenade in front of her peers without the hardback edition of the *Collins Book of Birds* falling off her noddle.

Anyhow, here is a quick rundown of the basics. I've devoted another whole section to the proper way to get out of a car without showing your pants. Otherwise, these pointers are pretty straightforward and easy to grasp.

BEARING

Posture is vital to get right. Shuffling around in a plastic rain hat and grandma coat with a Sainsbury's carrier bag in each hand is guaranteed to make you look bad, but compound it by slumping forwards and staring at your feet, and you'll never impress the Duke.

The general principle is to stand erect: shoulders back, stomach in, bum in, back and neck straight but not rigid. Ears, shoulders, hips, knees and ankles should be of columnar straightness. A plumb line hung from your earlobe should pass right through the middle of your ankle.

See page 86 for advice on high heels, which will help you to stand straight.

CONDUCT

1   Don't eat with your elbows on the table. Your mum was right.
2   When eating soup, tip bowl and spoon *away* from yourself.
3   Affect confidence and look people in the eye when you talk to them.
4   Don't point with your finger, not because it's rude but because it is masculine. Use your whole hand or incline your head in the intended direction. Imitate the way the women do it on the weather forecast.
5   An instruction from 1845 which still applies today: *never scratch your head, pick your teeth, clean your nails, or worst of all, pick your nose in company; all these things are disgusting. Spit as little as possible – and never upon the floor.* That last is particularly important. If there's one golden rule, more important than all the others put together, it's *that* one.

❈ *Burping is also known as belching, ructus, or eructation.* ❈

How to
Shave Your Legs Properly

During the Elizabethan age, a shaved forehead and eyebrows were all the rage and, together with her gorgeous long black teeth Elizabeth I sported a famously high forehead which she may have shaved to accommodate those tall wigs. I don't know what her legs looked like because they were always under her skirts plugged into a pair of fine silk stockings, which in 1560 she liked, 'so well, because they are pleasant, fine and delicate, that henceforth I will wear no more cloth stockings'. But I have the feeling that Liz's lallies were unshaved and looked a bit like Beryl the Peril's in tights, or maybe even Desperate Dan's naked.

The modern trend for bald legs and armpits really took off in America (of course) in the May 1915 edition of *Harper's Bazaar*, which pictured a model with hairless underarms in a sleeveless evening gown. By the 1920s razor companies were running campaigns to persuade flappers that hirsuteness was unfeminine and over successive decades, with rising hemlines and increasingly visible lower limbs, women reached more and more for the razor. During the Second World War, a shortage of nylons led to young ladies shaving their legs so as to facilitate the simulation of stocking seams by nifty use of the eyebrow pencil.

In olden days a glimpse of stocking was looked on as something shocking, now, heaven knows, the sky's the limit and the celebrity trend for waxing anything that moves has resulted in the nowadays commonplace 'Brazilian' (partial) and 'Hollywood' (total) below-the-belt depilation.

But let's stick to old fashioned legs for the moment. There are a few tips that will make the shaving experience nicer for you, though I can't promise that a man in a Ferrari will instantaneously whisk you off to a romantic dinner the moment you've finished. Indeed, I'm reminded of Deana Carter's lugubrious song *Did I shave my legs for this?* But never mind, we might as well be hopeful, so here are the vitals.

1   Use a really good razor. Go for the big brands.
2   Exfoliate before shaving: exfoliation – the removal of dead skin – can prevent ingrowing hairs. It also makes your pins *look* better.
3   Soak your legs for at least three minutes before shaving: water softens the hair.
4   Use a proper thick shaving gel or foam (men's works as well as women's). Soap is insufficiently lubricious, but hair conditioner will do the job nicely.
5   Rinse your razor after each stroke.
6   Change razor often.
7   Work from the ankles up for the closest shave unless your skin is irritated by shaving, in which case shave in the direction of hair growth.
8   Shave slowly, there's no hurry.

9   Mind out round your ankles, it's easy to nick yourself. Styptic pencil!
10 Always moisturize afterwards.

❀ *The leg's interosseous membrane separates its front and back muscles.* ❀

How to
Give Yourself a Brazilian Wax

Named after the country where it originated, the Brazilian wax is an especially thoroughgoing bikini wax, informally known as the 'G-wax' or plain 'Brazilian'. It differs from the common-or-garden bikini wax in that practically all the hair is removed from the pubic and bumular area, with just a narrow strip being left behind, like a wisteria blossom over the front door. It's important not to confuse the Brazilian with the so-called 'Hollywood', 'Sphynx' or 'smoothie', which is a total slash-and-burn wax.

Arab, Turkish and Persian women as well as Albanian and Mediterranean ladies have been waxing like gooduns for centuries, and there is now even a male version called the 'boyzilian' or, charmingly, 'back, crack and sack'. The ancients used sugar-based waxes for their waxes, but you will be using a wax-based wax.

You can purchase kits all over the place, which use either hard or soft wax. With soft wax, a muslin or cotton strip is pressed firmly on top of the wax and pulled off once it has cooled. The hard-wax technique requires no strips – you just hang on to the hardened (still pliable) wax and pull. Whereas soft wax can be sticky and leave behind a residue, hard wax will not do this and is therefore gentler and less painful, gripping the hair without adhering to the skin.

The first time you do a Brazilian wax, take a couple of painkillers half an hour before. This will ease things a little. Some waxees report mild post-wax 'Brazilian itch' (or 'Britch') but it's otherwise an innocuous process. Remember though: never re-apply wax to an already waxed area. Ouch!

Here's the way to create the perfect bikini wax in the privacy of your home, and at a fraction of the cost of a salon visit. Start at the front and move towards the back, not forgetting to leave a little landing strip, as described. You'll need to adopt all sorts of odd positions to get at everything but do not be tempted to cut corners by using gaffer tape. The results can be unsightly.

All right then girls, good luck – and chocks away!

REQUIRED
* *Proprietary bikini waxing kit (hard wax recommended)*
* *A microwave oven*
* *A few wooden or plastic spatulas (not kitchen size – smallish)*

INSTRUCTIONS
1   Have a shower and trim the hair. You only need about $\frac{1}{4}$in for the wax to grab hold of.
2   Heat the (hard) wax in the microwave according to the instructions. Stir until it's thick and honey-like but don't allow it to get too hot or you'll hurt yourself. Test the temperature with a finger before you put any of it on to your bikini area.
3   Using a spatula, apply a thick layer of wax in the direction of hair growth and allow it to cool for half a minute or so, until it is still pliable – follow the instructions on the label.
4   Now for the moment of truth: hold the skin taut and pull the wax away in one swift motion against the direction of growth, thus tearing the hairs out by their roots. Oh dear, just thinking about it makes your eyes water, doesn't it.
5   Immediately apply firm pressure to the waxed area with fingers or palm so as to lift off any remaining particles of wax.

6   Finally, tweeze out any stray hairs.
7   Once you've finished, spread a soothing lotion over waxed areas.

Waxing should take between 20 and 30 minutes and will last up to two months before stubble appears, allowing you to wear a minimalistic bikini without having to worry about taking a comb along to the beach. In this respect it's better than shaving, which will have you scratching like a squirrel within a couple of hours.

❀ *Brazil is the 5th largest country in the world.* ❀

How to
Lose Six Pounds in Six Hours

*M*aybe you've got an impending weekly weigh-in at the diet club or someone's sprung a blind date on you for tonight and you simply *must* get into those jeans that, at the best of times, require you to lie on the floor and writhe into them while two friends with pliers stand by ready to close the zip. If that's the case, here's the answer.

Level one
* *Sauna (often good for a pound or two)*
* *Diuretics (dandelion, nettle tea)*
* *Cut hair short*
* *Dress light: no belt (obviously), sandals, diaphanous dress*

Level two
* *Glasses off*
* *Wear cheap air-filled flip-flops instead of those huge great heavy sandals*
* *Remove all jewellery, including tiny earrings, nose piercing and wedding ring*
* *Cut hair extremely short*
* *Give blood (an armful weighs quite a lot). Refuse tea and biscuits!*

* *Swap big knickers for tiny thong, crotchless knickers, or net bikini bottoms*
* *Bra off*

LEVEL THREE (DESPERATE LAST-FEW-OUNCE MEASURES)

* *Cut or bite toe and fingernails right down*
* *Pluck eyebrows*
* *Shave legs*
* *Do a Brazilian wax (see page 127)*
* *Turn up in g-string (or go commando), and bare feet*
* *Remove makeup*
* *Blow nose*
* *Pick scabs*
* *Clean ears*
* *Shave any remaining body hair*
* *Read something sad and have a good cry*
* *Shave head*
* *Exfoliate. Twice*
* *Squeeze spots*
* *File hard skin from bottom of feet*
* *Spit*
* *Breath out last lungful of air before getting on the scales – tiny droplets of water vapour escaping may just tip the scales in your favour.*

Failing all these, have your legs amputated.

❀ *The parent company of Weight Watchers is H J Heinz.* ❀

How to
Make a Little Black Dress Out of a Bin Liner

The little black dress was invented by Coco Chanel in 1926 and has been fantastically popular for more than 80 years. Asked once by journalists about her creation Ms Chanel commented: 'Scheherazade is easy. The little black dress is hard.' This reminds me of one of those quotes they put in A level papers and then say, 'Discuss,' leaving you stunned and speechless owing to the utter vacuity of the material. I think even I A Richards would have had his work cut out making sense of that one.

The LBD is always flattering and suits almost any occasion or venue, from cocktail party to casino. It can be worn by anyone, knowing no social, style or size boundaries and like all the classics its secret is simplicity. It can be serious, chic *and* sexy, and will outlast all your trendy frocks without itself ever going out of style. You can even add jewellery, from pearls to paste to plastic and it will still look good. To fashion one from a bin liner in an emergency, just follow these simple steps.

REQUIRED
* *2 bin liners*
* *Sellotape*
* *Sharp scissors*
* *Gaffer tape*

INSTRUCTIONS
1 Turn the bin liner bottom-up and cut a hole in the middle, large enough for your head to fit through.
2 Cut the front artistically into a scoop, or V-neck. Keep your cuts smooth and flowing; you want a clean line, not lots of little snippy snips.
3 Cut armholes at each side to produce the classic sleeveless sheath. The holes should be large enough to allow your arms to slip through comfortably without cutting off the circulation and turning them white and cold. For the busy housewife, those bin liners with the black handles at the sides are a godsend, providing ready-made neckline and armholes. All you need to do is cut the bottom out for your legs. But beware of bin liners with a white plastic drawstring, which are neither use nor ornament.

4   Decorate the shoulder seam with a wide 6in strip cut from another bin liner. Tie into a small bow at each shoulder. *Note*: less is more. When it comes to bows think Jackie Kennedy not Margaret Thatcher.

5   Nip the dress in at the waist with a couple of lengths of doubled-over bin liner taped together to form a belt. This is easier if you have it on at the time. Don't attempt to approach the project like a tailor with a bit of chalk. You can't chalk a shiny bin liner.

6   The dress should be knee-length. For the hemline there is a choice of classy finishes:

    (A) a straight slit up one side or up the back.

    (B) tapered length, higher at the front than the back or higher on one side than the other.

For that Liz Hurley look, cut a hole for your head as above then split the bin liner down each side seam from the shoulder (use a sharp knife or scissors. You don't want a raggedy old tear). Place the dress over your head, and securely tape the seams closed at the side, using strips of gaffer tape in an accent colour (maybe matching your handbag or lippy). This will produce a flesh-revealing gap – so make sure you put the tape on such that you cover all the bits you'd prefer to keep under wraps.

*   Keep legs bare or wear sheer stockings.

*   Add classic earrings, and maybe a minimal silver or gold necklace or some pearls. The little black dress is made for teaming with your accessories.

*   Do not iron.

         ❀ *'Coco' Chanel's real name was Gabrielle.* ❀

V

Powder-Puff Mechanics

*Essential fast-lane skills for
girls with attitude*

*I didn't fight to get women out from behind the vacuum cleaner
to get them on to the board of Hoover.*

GERMAINE GREER

How to
Do a Handbrake Turn

*T*he handbrake turn is a driving technique used to reduce your car's turning circle on a tight bend or to quickly flick the car around 180° so it is travelling the opposite way: a quick change of direction without the need for a three-point turn. It is not difficult but requires practice to do safely and well. The effect is accomplished by pulling on the handbrake so that it 'locks' the rear wheels, creating a deliberate skid. As soon as the car is pointing the right way, you release the brake and zoom off.

It's ideal for impressing men or for intimidating fearsome mothers-in-law. So on with the crash helmet and away you go.

Instructions

1   Find a smooth open space without obstacles.

2   Drive forwards at about 30mph in first or second gear.

3   Ease off on the accelerator, depress the clutch and quickly twist the steering wheel to the right with your right hand until it locks. (You can turn to the left by doing the opposite.)

4   Immediately the turn begins, pull the handbrake on with your left hand, keeping the button depressed during the turn. The rear wheels will lock and the back of the car will skid out to the left (in this case). You'll really feel the G-force as it spins out.

5   As you're spinning, gradually bring the steering wheel back to the centre.

6   To limit the rotation – if required – apply the foot brake. This will also stop any movement of the car backwards. If you can't straighten up, and just keep spinning round and round, it's called – humiliatingly – 'a doughnut'.

7   The moment you are pointing in the intended direction, release the handbrake and *brrrrrmmmmm!* you're off and away. If only one could do a handbrake turn in life sometimes.

Important tips

* A handbrake turn is easiest in a front-wheel-drive car, though any car will do.
* In a rear-wheel drive manual car, you must also depress the clutch to avoid stalling the engine.
* Don't perform handbrake turns on a public road. Practise on a disused airfield or somewhere with a smooth tarmac surface.
* If it has just rained or snowed, that will help.
* Repeated handbrake turns ruin your tyres and make your hands dry. A good moisturizer is essential.

❀ It takes longer to begin braking if you are listening to music. ❀

Parallel Parking for Ladies

*A*s E B White once pointed out: 'Everything in life is somewhere else, and you get there in a car.' So unless you want another person to do all the parking for you, you'd better learn. When my Uncle Bob was teaching me he told me: 'You never really learn to swear until you learn to parallel park.' Just what is it that's so tricky? Maybe it's the going backwards thing. I remember my mum reversing into a gigantic double-decker coach once, covered in balloons. When my dad asked her how, in an otherwise deserted car park and the name of God, she had managed to home in like a heat-seeking missile on this enormous charabanc, she responded memorably: 'I didn't see it.' Anyway, here, in case you are one of those who finds parallel parking a sort of going backwards with knobs on, is the low-down.

INSTRUCTIONS

When you are parking, there are a couple of things to remember. Don't get too close to the parked car on your left and don't mount the pavement. But do try to stop close enough that you won't need to walk half a mile to the kerb. Always use your mirror, and signal your intentions, keeping a constant lookout for passing traffic. You can stop the car at any time during the manoeuvre.

1   Halt your car parallel to a stationery car with a space behind it. A friend of mine who has passed the advanced driving test says he simply won't attempt parallel parking unless the gap is more than $1^{1}/_{2}$ times the length of his own car. This is an excellent piece of advice that I always follow. The more space, the easier it is. Anyway, you should have pulled up next to, and no more than three feet away from, the car on your left.

2   Engage reverse gear and look all around, including in the rear-view mirror, to check that it's safe to move. Drive straight back very slowly and watch out for the rear driver's-side corner of the stationery car as it becomes visible, over your shoulder, through the side window.

3   As soon as it does, and if things are clear, turn the steering wheel to the left *one whole turn*. This will cause the front of your car to swing out on the driver's side, turning your car diagonally.

4   If it is still safe, continue to move backwards until the front of your car is next to the famous back corner of the car next door. At this point, turn the steering wheel fully to the right. This will make the front of your car swing to the left, into the kerb. Watch carefully to make sure that you are not going to tear the side off the stationery vehicle. Any ear-splitting rending sounds or metallic

shrieking like fingernails down a blackboard will let you know that you are probably a bit too close.

5   You should now be close to both the kerb and the car next door, so your fight-or-flight hormones will be pumping away like mad, and you may start to pant and glow. Continue to move the car very slowly backwards into position, turning the wheel to the left just a little at a time, to prevent you swinging in too far and getting jammed. Keep an eye on your distance from both kerb and car. If you sense resistance, you are probably against the kerb though it might equally well be a tree, plastic rubbish bin or pillar box. You can't win this fight, so move forwards a bit and try again.

6   You should now be parallel with and close enough to the kerb – but not too close. If you need to adjust your position, you can move forwards and backwards to get it right (the easy bit).

At all times you need to remember that vehicles may be coming from the front and from behind. Swinging out suddenly into moving traffic is a bad idea. As is reversing into large balloon-covered coaches.

❀ *A single yellow line means, 'No waiting during times shown on sign'.* ❀

How to
Escape a Vicious Swarm of Bees

INSTRUCTIONS

*   Bees normally attack only when threatened – take care if you are around a nest or a hive. Once they do sting, a pheromone is released that rouses other healthy, grown-up busy, busy bees which then go into defence mode, stinging away merrily. The first thing to do is get out of there. Kick off high heels or other unsuitable footwear and run as fast as you can. Probably, the best place to head for is the inside of a building. But don't forget to shut the door behind you. Your common-or-garden honeybee will probably give up chasing you after about 150 feet ($1\frac{1}{2}$ times the length of a netball court), but African honeybees will go three times this far – $4\frac{1}{2}$ netball courts.

* Bees will instinctively go for your head so, as you flee, try to cover your face with whatever you have to hand (not golden syrup or Ribena obviously, I mean something like a blanket or a jacket).

* Running through bushes is a good way to slow up swarming bees, and a wind will make it harder for them too. Switching on a leaf blower and blasting them with it is worth a try but one tends to be too preoccupied with running and screaming to do much else in these bee escapades. If you must scream, keep your mouth closed. Being stung on or in the mouth may cause a swelling that can block your airway.

* *Important warning*: never jump into water, because although bees are rotten swimmers they are excellent hoverers and will probably be waiting for you when you come up, gasping for air.

* If (when) you do get stung, remove the sting as quickly as you can by raking your finger nail or your credit card across it. Unlike wasps, bees commit suicide when they sting, releasing a poison sac that continues its muscular pumping action outside the bee's body for as much as 10 minutes. Unless you are seriously allergic to bee venom (in which case you might go into anaphylactic shock, a life-threatening medical emergency causing rapid constriction of the airway) you are unlikely to suffer serious harm, even if you are stung several times.

* Ice, antihistamine pills and calamine lotion all work pretty well on a non-allergic sting. In most cases, the pain will disappear within a couple of hours, though the swelling may only become visible the next day. Also recommended is a glass of wine and a sit-down.

❀ *Pristine honey has been found alongside the ancient mummies of the pharaohs.* ❀

How to
Force a Cucumber

*T*he friendly cucumber (*cucumis sativus*) is a fast-growing subtropi-cal vine, related to the melon. Cucumbers have been cultivated for 3,000 years and come in more than 100 varieties, from pickle-size to monster Zeppelins. My Uncle Vivian used to force cucumbers in the south-facing conservatory of his Regency house in Brighton. His cucumber sandwiches were models of their kind, coming sans-crust and on a silver thing like three flying saucers on a stick.

FORCING AND HOTBEDS

'Forcing' is just a word that refers to the acceleration of growth result-ing from the application of additional heat, and with a bit of tender loving care you can force your own cucumbers under glass. Frame, greenhouse or hotbed specimens can reach 18 inches within two or three months so long as you keep them nice and warm, and feed and water them regularly. (A hotbed is a low mound of earth covered by glass, and heated by rotting manure.)

SOWING, GERMINATION AND PLANTING

Sow your cukes in late February or early March, putting each seed sideways, ½in deep, into a little peat pot containing seed compost. Raise your seedlings under glass and keep them warm: 70–80° F / 21–26° C is a must. They will germinate after four or five days. Plant them out, one per pot, two per growing bag – late March in a heated greenhouse, late May in an unheated one, or under a frame. After planting, water them in and keep the compost moist, feeding if neces-sary. Never let your vines wilt.

TENDER LOVING CARE

1   Keep your cucumbers at a minimum of 60° F / 15° C in full sun if possible. The compost should be high in organic matter and moist but never waterlogged, so water frequently in small amounts. Keep

the air moist and well ventilated (think sub-tropical). You can do this in a hot greenhouse by spraying the floor. Don't spray the vines.

2 Train the stem up a wire, cane or trellis. When the main stem reaches the roof, pinch it out at the top. Pinch out also the tip of each side shoot two leaves beyond the female flower. Female flowers produce the fruit and are recognizable by the infant cucumber behind them.

3 Pick off all the male flowers (boring job), which you can recognize because they have no fruit, just a stalk. Fertilized cucumbers taste bitter.

4 Pinch out the tips of flowerless side shoots when they reach a length of 2ft.

5 Once the first cucumbers have started to swell, feed your vines with a good tomato fertilizer every two weeks.

Harvest

So long as you pick the fruit before they over-ripen and turn yellow, your vines will bear cukes aplenty: up to 25 per vine. You can harvest them at whatever size you like, once they are looking less round and their sides have lost the bulge. If they begin to turn yellow, they've gone too far and will taste bitter and dry. Don't pull them off, cut them. Frequent picking encourages prolific blossoming and more fruit. The smell of the blossom is just beautifully cucumbery.

❋ *The world's largest cucumber weighed in at 59lbs.* ❋

How to
Make a Compost Heap

Right then, before we start, do we know what we're talking about? What exactly is compost? The word comes from the Latin *composita* 'something put together', which gives you a good idea that a pile of twigs with an old settee on the top, or a heap of grass cuttings leaking a virulent brown ooze are not really compost. You need a balance of decayed organic material before you will get anything that is a good fertilizer for your rhubarb.

The best compost is made by putting vegetable matter (say hay) into one end of a compost generator (say, a horse) and collecting it at the other end not long afterwards. This is the also the quickest way.

To produce the compost in a heap, you must provide air, water and nitrogen to the aerobic (oxygen-loving) bacteria and fungi so they can break down the plant cellulose. The more nitrogen in your compost heap the quicker the rot and the greater the heat – a useful by-product that kills off the weeds.

* *Air*: comes in from gaps in your compost heap.
* *Water*: a bit of rain or a regular dose of dishwater in hot weather will be enough.
* *Nitrogen*: good sources are animal manure, urine, fishmeal and blood.
* *Carbon*: plant cellulose (say twigs, cabbage leaves and £5 notes).

The bacteria you need are already there in the garden but if you use animal manure, you'll be adding some extra.

THE COMPOST LOO
One of the niftiest compost heaps is the straw loo.

1 Tie a load of dry straw stalks in a barrel-size bunch and stand them in the garden, upright like an dustbin.
2 Whenever you need to, simply pee on top of the straw. This process is less scratchy for gentlemen. Gravity and capillary action will distribute the nitrogen and water amongst the carbon stalks, where air and time will work together with the garden bugs to decompose the plant cellulose. You'll see the steam from the reaction on cold mornings. It's odour-free and fun for visitors too.

THE TRADITIONAL COMPOST HEAP

1   Lay several rows of bricks, leaving gaps between.

2   Overlay sticks or slim branches perpendicular to the bricks, to let air in underneath.

3   Nail together four wooden pallets or ask a man. Pallets are ideal, having gaps in the side that let in the air. Leave one side as a loose 'door' for easy compost removal in due time.

4   Build the heap by sprinkling a 10in layer of vegetable matter. Don't include too much woody material; it takes ages to rot down. You need a balance of soft and hard (peelings, fruit, grass-cuttings, last year's tax disk, a few bark chippings), followed by a couple inches of nitrogen-rich stuff – manure for preference.

5   Water regularly in dry weather.

6   Keep the layers going all season, paying attention to the balance of plant matter. Don't throw on any meat, eggs (washed shells are OK), your mother-in-law or other animal matter that will attract foxes or vermin.

7   At the end of the season stop for the winter.

8   In February or March open your compost 'door' and dig out the compost from the bottom. Chuck round your runner beans and raspberries and over your delphiniums and daisies.

❀ *Gertrude Jekyll created more than 400 gardens.* ❀

How to
Test Pearls for Genuineness

Genuine pearls are classed as 'natural' or 'cultured'. Natural pearls are formed when a small foreign object becomes embedded in an oyster. The mollusc secretes a mixture of crystalline and organic substances called nacre, which builds in protective layers around the irritant, eventually forming a pearl. Cultured pearls are natural in all respects except their inception, whereby a foreign object is deliberately introduced to provoke the pearl-forming process. Nowadays, more than 95% of the world's pearls are cultured.

Fake pearls, in contrast, are made by coating a plastic or mother-of-pearl core with a paint containing ground fish scales, or pearly-looking plastic.

Even these paste gewgaws will take people's minds off your wrinkles in a low light, but if you want to find out the true worth of a pearl necklace some gentleman has just given you then, girls, you gotta test 'em. Good fakes can be hard to spot these days but you can try the following.

* *Tooth test*: rub the pearl delicately along the biting edge of your top front gnashers. Pearls are made mostly of calcium carbonate ($CaCO_3$) and the genuine article will feel gritty or sandy, whereas a synthetic pearl will feel smooth. This is the easiest way to test a pearl but it's rather rough and ready so don't rely on it if you are a newcomer to the world of pearl chewing.
* *Magnification test*: examine the pearl's surface with a strong magnifying glass. Real pearls look smooth and finely granulated while imitations appear more coarsely grainy.
* *Necklace-hole test*: examine the hole with a lens. The edges of the hole will be sharp and crisp in a genuine pearl and may even be chipped. The hole will be blobby and irregular in an imitation.
* *Weight test*: gently bounce the pearls in your hand. They will feel dense and heavy if real, and light and insubstantial if fake – unless they are made of glass.
* *Blemish test*: look closely for flaws in the surface. Real pearls will have a variety of natural irregularities in their surface. If your pearls are flawless and look too good to be true they probably are.

PEARLY NAMES
The name Margarita means 'pearl' as do Margaret, Peggy, Marjorie, Margot, Maggie, Gretchen, Greta, Gretel and Rita. They signify purity, humility, innocence and sweetness.

Most notably, of course, the name Pearl means 'pearl'. I think it's time for one of my tablets.

❀ Hänsel und Gretel *(1893) is an opera by Engelbert Humperdinck.* ❀

How to
Bluff a Tradesman

Most women I know feel like fish out of water whenever they have to instruct a tradesman. The problem is twofold in that tradesmen (A) understand their trade and you don't, and (B) are men. This means you have the talking-to-a-man-about-technical-things-you-don't-really-understand problem.

My brother was arguing with me yesterday about how they make the maps work behind the weather forecasters on the telly. He maintained that presenters must choose the colour of their clothes with care to avoid 'disappearing'. I said they more likely choose them to match their eyes. He said arguing with me was like trying to fold an airmail copy of *The International Herald Tribune* in a high wind.

The main thing to remember is that men and women talk in different ways. For a woman, 2am is the perfect time for a discussion about where our relationship is going. For a man, 2am is time for sleep. And when all you want is to unload your troubles over a glass of wine, women offer sympathy, men offer a solution. So when a mechanic tersely contradicts you about your clutch he is probably not being deliberately nasty. Similarly, when you ask a tiler to please make sure he arranges the multicoloured tiles sensitively, you will probably be met with a blank village-idiot look. With this in mind, here are some thoughts about how best to instruct a tradesman.

* Despite the heading at the top, don't bluff. This is the key to winning in this relationship. If you don't know, ask.
* Be clear about exactly what you want and check that it's been done. Remember, you hold the purse strings.

* Don't bang on the walls of a house you are about to buy. It doesn't tell you a darn thing and reveals you to be a likely pushover.
* Never kick the tyres of a car you are thinking of buying, for similar reasons.
* If you find yourself having to park a Chelsea tractor in a tiny space after a test drive, don't! Get out and invite the salesman to do it.
* If you want your tiles done a certain way, stand there and micromanage him. He may be good at gluing them on but he's probably no Ostrogoth mosaicist.
* Thatchers do not welcome last-minute suggestions from you about interesting designs they could do by the chimney.
* Make up for your lack of technical knowledge with friendliness and sexy confidence. You can save hundreds of pounds like this.

❀ *80% of thatch used in Britain is imported.* ❀

How to
Change a Tyre Without Breaking a Nail

One foul day, I remember, I was driving across Dartmoor towards a wedding in Stoke Fleming. Squinting between the furiously swishing windscreen wipers, I recall going over a huge bump just as a flash of blue lighting lit up the moors, like in David Lean's *Oliver Twist* (1948). And then the car's steering seemed to go a bit weird.

Stopping beside some sheep, I craned my neck out and spotted at once that I had a flat tyre. Of course I was dressed in a new, lovely and expensive LRD (Little Red Dress) and now had to change a tyre in a tempestuous rainstorm. I am going to draw a veil over the remainder of that morning, which contained, I am ashamed to confess, an extravagance of profane rhetoric that would have frozen the marrow of Blackbeard's most fescennine brigand and caused his blood to run yellow.

In case you ever find yourself in a 'flat-tyre situation' here are a few tips so you can walk away with your nails all neat and tidy. Let's just hope you never have to do it in the rain.

REQUIRED
* *Car (obviously)*
* *Wheel brace. This is a lever, sometimes in a cross formation, with a spanner-type cup at the end for putting over the wheel nuts.*
* *A jack*
* *A rag*
* *Alcohol hand wipes*
* *Vaseline*
* *Gloves (vital)*

INSTRUCTIONS

1 As soon as you are aware of the flat, drive to a safe place, as slowly as you dare on the punctured tyre. If you're on the motorway avoid changing the wheel on the hard shoulder. Instead, use an emergency phone and call for help. On a main road, find a lay-by. But even here, be aware of the traffic. I was once nearly hit by a flying scaffolding pole that came off a lorry.

2   Having stopped on a well-lit level surface, switch off and put the car into reverse. Put on the handbrake and hazard lights.

3   Now, remove any heavy luggage or dead bodies from the boot.

4   Take off your shoes if they are fancy. *You shouldn't have been driving in those.*

5   Smear your hands with a light coating of Vaseline and put on the gloves. These can be wool, leather or whatever. I keep a pair of suede gardening gauntlets in the boot as well as some tight-fitting Marigolds. If you need to protect your dress, try putting your coat on back-to-front.

6   Take the spare tyre out/off. Now is often the time that you notice: (A) there is no spare, or (B) it's flat. Jump up and down with rage, screaming at the top of your voice. There's little else you can do. If you're lucky enough to find the spare, you are going to have a jolly time lifting it out – it's extremely heavy.

7   Remove the tools. No jack? No wheel brace? Time for more blood-curdling screams and a mental note to have a polite word with your man.

8   Consult your handbook for detailed instructions and locate the correct lifting point nearest the wheel you are to replace. Don't jack at any other point; the car may collapse, seriously damaging the bodywork and taking your foot off.

9   If it's covering the wheel nuts, lever off the hubcap with the wheel brace.

10 Loosen the nuts by half a turn. Be aware that the nuts are often tightened in the garage by a machine. If they are really stiff, stand on the brace to shift them. If this doesn't work, try jumping up and down on it.

11 Use the jack to lift the car. Once the body is up, but before the wheel is off the ground, push the spare underneath to provide a safety cushion in case the car slips off the jack. A car can easily do this, even on a flat surface, so *never get under a car that is jacked up*.

12 Keep lifting and once the wheel is just clear of the road unscrew the nuts in diagonal pairs. I use my *rubber* gloves for this, otherwise I

can't feel what I'm doing. Put the nuts in your handbag or hat so they don't roll away or fall down a drain. Wrap them in a bit of old paper or tissue so they don't make your stuff filthy. Keep wiping everything with the rag as you go – it helps *you* to stay clean.

13 Remove the wheel. Three little words that sound so simple. This is a hell of a job on your own because the wheel is enormously heavy, and also filthy. It was hard enough getting the spare out of the car; this is much more difficult. Once it's off, heave it beside the new one, under the car.

14 Now wrestle the spare into place. More grunting, groaning and quiet cursing under your breath. Is it is the right way round? If not take it off and do it again. (This is awful, isn't it?) Replace the wheel nuts in diagonal pairs and finger-tighten them.

15 Jack the car down until the new tyre just touches the road. Then tighten the nuts a little more with the brace.

16 Drag the flat from underneath and finish lowering the car. Remove the jack and fully tighten the wheel nuts, jumping on the brace if you like. Put the damaged wheel in the boot: more heaving, finger pinching and medical-student-type swearing. Replace the filthy tools and pop the hubcap or plastic cover back on the wheel.

17 Throw the gloves into the boot and remove the Vaseline from your hands with a couple of alcohol wipes. They should come up a treat, and no broken nails. OK, your hair's a mess, your dress is ruined and your face is black. But your nails are perfect.

18 Get the tyre replaced as soon as you can.

❈ *Giovanni Battista Pirelli founded Pirelli & C. in Milan, In 1872.* ❈

How to
Get a Spider Out of the Bath

One glorious spring day last March, when the blackbirds were whistling in the magnolia, I got an email – it would once have been a letter – from somebody called sam.woodyard. It was a name I immediately recognized as that of an old schoolfriend about whom I'd heard nothing for more than a thousand years – or several decades anyway. Samantha's father had started as tea-boy in a small lock-smith's shop (small shop, not small locksmith) and worked his way up, turning the business into a multi-million-pound security concern, and becoming MD. This was the time when everybody didn't keep changing job, school, house, country, husband and haircut – a time when starting at the bottom and working your way up was a good way to get on.

Anyway, as I recalled his daughter across the graves of the days I remembered a svelte, sparkling, lithe and willowy beauty who was going to become an actress. We arranged to meet at Victoria station, but when she turned up she was a huge fat woman quite unlike the sylph of remembrance, her gross waddling toes swathed in carpet slip-pers, her blotty yellow sausage-legs telling of a life spoiled by malady and defeat. She greeted me with, 'Nice to see you, to see you nice,' possibly the most meaningless and annoying catchphrase ever. She had changed.

The only reason I'm going into all this is that Samantha was one of the few girls I knew who would happily dispose of the horrible, huge, brown, hairy-legged spiders that skulked rebarbatively in the school baths. These are a few of her methods.

* *Violence*: use a tennis racket, towel or other object to whack or smash the thing into oblivion. But mind the glass bottles.
* *Ask a man*: if you have a chap to hand, try asking him. The problem is that men seem just as prone to the willies as women, so it's a bit hit and miss, this one. Best go on to the others.
* *Gadget*: spider-catcher gizmos are available. But don't then wash it down the drain; it will shake itself dry and be out the plug hole again before you can say octopod.
* *Spray*: use an aerosol insecticide (aracnicide). Failing that, hair-spray will 'freeze' its legs into position so it can't scuttle up the chain.

✱   *Flannel method*: squash the thing. If you don't like getting up close, throw the flannel at it first to stun it and finish it off with the loofah.

❀   *The loofah is a tropical vine fruit, not a kind of sponge.*   ❀

How to
Manage an Umbrella in the Wind

*H*andling an umbrella in the wind is as hazardous today as it looks as if it was in Edwardian times, though the modern instrument is different. When I was small, umbrellas were still beautiful things and a pleasure to use, though just as today you couldn't buy one that started shrieking if you left it on a train. My grandfather used to get his from a supplier near the British Museum. Black, sleek, and pointed they were, with a yellow cane handle like the knobbly finger of an arthritic wizard. The modern equivalent is a collapsible plastic article that only lasts through a couple of rainstorms.

Opening an umbrella in the wind demands skill. If you are not careful you are likely to put somebody's eye out with one of those little blobs on the end of the spokes. People often leap away in alarm, sometimes bumping other passers-by or jumping into the road, causing mayhem and car crashes. But you mustn't worry about them because you will have your hands full, fighting something like a cross between an angry black swan and a kite. Here are a few tips.

INSTRUCTIONS

1   For a start, always open the umbrella with the wind blowing towards you. If the wind is behind you it will simply blow the thing inside out with an enormous whoof! Not only is this hard to recover from but you look ridiculous.

2   Once it's open keep the umbrella facing into the wind. In a gale this will mean pushing it before you like a shield, with its umbrel-

lorial axis near the horizontal. You are now effectively blind and will run into people with the sharp point (if it has a sharp point). The worst thing is two blind horizontal-brolly holders meeting each other going in opposite directions. Let us draw a veil over the scene.

3   A sudden sharp change in wind direction can catch you off guard. A lady of my acquaintance was once picked up and carried over a low wall as she clung desperately on to what had become, effectively, a parasail. If you find the wind suddenly behind you, simply fling the umbrella down into the gutter. Better safe than sorry.

4   After a rainstorm, never stand with your umbrella open, dripping dry. I once saw a humourist drop ping-pong balls and cotton wool into a lady's open brolly at a bus stop, followed by a lighted match.

Seeing the smoke, she flailed the thing around, thus fanning the fire enough to ignite the umbrella's skin. It was quite a show, I can tell you.

5   If all this sounds too much like hard work, get yourself one of those see-through folded-up rain hats that tie under the chin. Very ageing but easier.

❈ *The scent from dry earth following a shower is petrichor, a plant oil.* ❈

How to
Meet Your Ex's New Girlfriend

Once, as the guest of an old beau, I attended a wedding reception where I was seated with some of his other exes. I say 'some' but in fact there were 11 of us, occupying two huge tables. And what a lively lot we were; the laughter was simply raucous, provoked chiefly by our swapping of stories about this particular gentleman's – how shall I put it? – *foibles*. Yes, that's it. We all felt a bit sorry for the bride that day, partly because of the sheer number of us, to all of whom she had to be introduced, but also because we each knew what was in store for the poor girl.

Meeting your ex's new flame is always a slightly weird and often tense occasion. Will she be: prettier, cleverer, of better family, more charming, sexier – with a superlative hourglass figure? Will she have the three things most notoriously of importance to a girl: breeding, brains and beauty. Is she, in short, a willowy Nordic princess who is a professional model and pin-up with degrees from Oxbridge, Harvard and the Sorbonne? Secretly, of course, you hope she will be a witless, lumpen ne'erdowell, with flies buzzing round her toothless head, anorak and dungarees. Unfortunately, she is usually a lovely girl of great charm and intelligence. Which is only to be expected really. After all, your ex has good taste: that's why he chose you. But that doesn't stop you feeling feelings of *unfavourable* comparison the whole time.

Anyway it's time to gird your loins. Prepare for the worst but hope for the best, and take whatever comes. Here are a few tips.

* Always start off with grace and style (keep your powder dry, though, just in case).
* When you meet her, make sure it's on your own terms. If at all possible, you should have your new partner hanging on your arm (or hire an escort).
* It's sometimes better if your new man doesn't know that this fellow is your ex. The subtle effect of this is to make your old flame and his new girlfriend feel insignificant when you airily introduce them, damning them with faint praise to the man on your arm – and getting her name and details a bit wrong in the process.
* Never look as if you've tried too hard but make sure your hair is good and that you're looking nice – and as tall as possible. (*See* how to descend a staircase in high heels, page 86).

If you harbour feelings of revenge:

* Turn up with a filthy (clear) plastic bag containing horrible images downloaded from disgusting websites featuring elderly grannies and animals, several pairs of grubby women's undergarments, a cheap wig, a Scout's uniform, a few dirty compacted handkerchiefs and a train-spotting magazine. Announce: 'Oh, you left some bits and bobs behind.'
* Then send your floridly gay friend over to greet him with: 'Where did you disappear to last night, you naughty naughty girl?'
* If meeting number 1 goes especially badly, arrange meeting number 2 for the back of an aeroplane, one mile up just before her first sky dive. Take scissors.

❀ *Nell Gwyn's real name was Eleanor.* ❀

How to
Pack for a Holiday Without Using More Than Five Large Suitcases

*H*ave you spotted that men and women are different? Me too. My brother Tom complained that if he told me he was leaving to join a cult in the Himalayas that insisted on non-stop orgies, cannibalism and random *involuntary* euthanasia, the first thing I would ask, like most women, would be: 'Oh, who will you be going with?' That is unfair since if he *was* planning to join such a sect, my first question would certainly be: 'Is that *all the luggage you're taking?!*' He was once questioned at length by the Minneapolis immigration authorities when they disbelieved his explanation that the tiny carry-on bag in his hand *was* his stuff for a three-month stay.

Whenever he does go on holiday he maintains, like most men, that one set of trousers and three or four shirts is enough for two weeks, and that in an emergency he can survive on just *one set of clothes* by using his patented overnight hotel-shower-and-radiator technique (don't ask). Unlike him, I like to pack enough to cover all the eventualities and, in the way of most women, I can recall every outfit I've worn on holiday over the past two decades. My brother can't remember what he had on yesterday without looking on the floor beside the bed.

Anyway, airlines are increasingly charging for baggage, so here are a few methods of avoiding extra costs.

* Take twice as much money as you planned and pack half as much stuff. Buy whatever you need when you get there.
* Remember, the less you take the more you can bring home. Just think of all those exciting shops.
* Don't take gallons of shampoo, conditioner, perfume and so forth. There is hardly a place in the world that doesn't have toiletries.

* Buy presents for your foreign hosts only once you get there. Generic pots, T-shirts and things can be authenticized with last-minute additions such as: *A gift from Europe's famous Britain* in indelible felt pen.

* Don't go mountaineering, skiing or on jungle or polar holidays, because you always need a vast amount of impedimenta. Instead plump for a hot beach location where a bikini and flip-flops will cover everything. Well, you know what I mean.

* Camper vans are a sort of travelling suitcase. Unless you are groovy, avoid the ones with flowers and rainbows painted on. You'll look silly clambering out the back in your high heels and pearls. Not very suitable in Venice either.

* Offer to pack your boyfriend's stuff with yours, then accidentally forget. Use the space for your own things.

* Shrink-wrap your clothes with one of those special vacuum machines. You can improvise with a hoover and a bin liner.

❋ *The British monarch does not carry a passport.* ❋

How to
Read a Map on a Car Journey

*T*here is a stereotypical idea that men read maps better than women – and it turns out to be true. We women tend to use landmarks to navigate, whereas men prefer to use the old fashioned and dull compass points: north, south, east and west, to find their way. They are also more likely to think in units of distance.

Typically, a woman will describe a journey like this: 'Go up past the new hairdressers that's where Tracy works now you know she's the lady with that funny dog and turn left by the Peter Pan fountain why doesn't somebody clean out all the litter they keep throwing in there and you'll see a big metal tank for water or is it gas it's something anyway by the place where Colin's mum with the built-up shoe had her accident then go past where the Russian vine went mad last year and then round a big roundabout and come off where there's a pretty hotel with a little bird table on the lawn and Grandma's house is right down the end of the terrace next to some flats with really high pink steps and a gnome showing his bottom outside.' Men are more likely to say something like: 'Go to the top, turn left and carry on for four minutes to a 48° dog-leg turn that'll take you north half a mile. Moloch Terrace is second exit – 11 o'clock – off the roundabout.'

Interestingly, a study at the University of East London found that *gay* men employ both male *and* female navigation techniques, whereas gay women read maps just like straight women. However, reading a map is supposed to be one of those things that women just can't do well. I certainly prefer to have the map facing the direction I'm going, turning it as we travel, which seems only sensible (tricky in a lift). Anyway, here are a few tips to help you next time you're navigating in the car.

* *Think like a man*: be short and sweet. Give numbers, times, compass points.
* *Learn the symbols*: it's a bit of a let-down if the driver and passengers discover that the navigator has been gaily following the River Kennet for the past half-hour, thinking it was the M4.
* *Use an up-to-date map*: anyone's navigation can be wrecked by a new road layout.
* *Shortcuts*: these are for people who *already know the way*. Otherwise they tend to extend journey times by about 20%.
* *The Observer's Book of Ley Lines*: these ancient putative lines of force are less likely to get you to your destination than water divining. Ordnance Survey maps may be boring but they really work.
* *Sat nav*: why not make everyone's life easier and invest in satellite navigation for your man's next birthday? Then you can enjoy the view or have a snooze instead.

❀ *Ordnance Survey has been making maps since 1791.* ❀

How to
Re-Point a Wall

When I was a girl my mum used to tell me to say please and thank you, always to take the smallest piece of cake and never to poke my tongue out at people. She also said it was rude to point. Of course she wasn't talking about filling the joints in the brickwork of a building, which is only rude when done by fatty builders with their bum cracks showing.

While converting your loft is probably something you want to get the experts in for, there's no reason you shouldn't be able to do a bit of re-pointing yourself. Don't expect your *giornata* to match Michelangelo's efforts, though, it's bound to look a bit ropey the first time you try it. Practise on an unobtrusive bit of wall round the back somewhere or on the home of an unliked neighbour before you dare move on to the Palladian brick frontage of Tabley House.

As well as smartening up a building's crumbling countenance, pointing is a valuable weatherproofing exercise. For example, if you've noticed damp penetration in your boudoir, and the pointing's all

Fig. B

Fig. A

dilapidated in the relevant place, then get out your trowel and you can kill two stones with one bird.

Anyway, here's how to go about re-pointing a wall.

REQUIRED
* *Hammer and chisel*
* *Watering can*
* *Sand and cement*
* *Pointing trowel*
* *Mortarboard (tasselless)*

INSTRUCTIONS

1   Whack out the old mortar to a depth of 1 inch, using a chisel. This is great fun. Better wear safety goggles though. I know they make you look silly but it can't be helped.

2   Clean the interstices with a brush, then soak the joints with water – the moisture helps your pointing to stick. A watering can works well but you might need to stand on a chair or ladder; gravity won't allow you to water upwards.

3   Make the mortar on a mixing board. It's a simple compound of sand and cement. Try some experiments with different combinations.

4   You can dye mortar in different colours to match your existing pointing. This can be fun, but for gawd's sake practise first to avoid producing ugsome monstrosities.

5   You must use the mortar within a couple of hours, before it hardens. This is a chemical process that won't work at very cold temperatures, when the water will freeze, leaving you with an uncompounded mush that just falls out.

6   Shape a trowelful of mortar into a wedge on your mortarboard (Fig. A).

7   With a pointing trowel (or a cake cutter in an emergency), scoop up a little mortar from the thin end of the wedge and push it into the wet joint. Beginners drop lots of it so put a sheet down or it will harden on the ground (Fig. B).

8   The pointing may be finished in different ways. So-called weather pointing projects slightly from the joint, like a little pitched roof, allowing rainwater to run off. You can accomplish this by running your trowel along the joint at an angle. If you want a concave profile, drag a piece of hose along the wet mortar. Or you can just rub it flush, which is good if the joints are especially tight.

9   Don't try to tackle large projects such as the British Library or the Great Pyramid of Keops until you've got a bit of practice under your belt. Or they'll be very cross with you.

❀ *The British Library contains more than 150 million items.* ❀

Understanding the Offside Rule

*T*here's this great cloud of unknowing about the offside rule in football. Even chaps seem a bit on the back foot when you tackle them about it. Did you notice how I got a *Daily Mirror*-style soccer metaphor in there, mixed though it might have been with a cricketing one? Anyway I sniffed around a bit in the new and excessively shiny Brighton public library so as to get to the bottom of this great mystery, and discovered within minutes that there's *nothing to* it.

For verification, I passed my findings around some male gentlemen of my acquaintance, including my Uncle Vivian and my Uncle Bob. Uncle Vivian demurred, telling me that his interest in football is entirely 'aesthetic', while Uncle Bob submitted an answer so opaque as to reveal only his exegetical inarticulacy.

However, I have studied this business from all angles now, such that I feel confident in asserting that I know of what I speak of – as the expert on pub signs explained to the Womens' Institute after a little too much pre-lecture Dutch courage down The Plough.

The offside rule was introduced to stop players hanging around the opponents' goal waiting for a long ball from the other end. The essence

Offside player

of it is that attacking players must not pass the ball forwards to team-mates who are further forward than any defender of the opposing team, *excluding the goalie.*

Three subtleties

1   You are not offside if you are level with the furthest defender.
2   You can't be offside in your own half.
3   You aren't offside if you receive the ball from a corner, throw-in or goal kick.

That's it in a nutshell. Next time there's any argument about it you can supply the authoritative explanation. I wouldn't expect any man to thank you for it though.

❀   *'I didn't see Pelé live, obviously, because I wasn't born.' David Beckham*   ❀

VI

Jolly Hockeysticks!

Smashing sports, hobbies
and pastimes for girls

Ducking for apples? Change one letter and it's the story of my life.

DOROTHY PARKER

How to
Do a Cartwheel

*D*uring my younger days I used to be quite acrobatic and cart-wheels were always my favourite. I remember doing a celebratory one in the public bar of the Queen's Head after my A levels, accidentally snapping a cigarette straight out of the mouth of an old man in a hat. He gave me such a look I just shrank. Anyway, indoors is probably not the place for cartwheels so the instructions below are for outside only. Jeans are the thing to wear when you are cartwheeling. Flapping skirts not only spoil the aesthetics – and blind you by falling over your face – but lay you open to accusations of exhibitionism.

INSTRUCTIONS

1 Empty your pockets of lip gloss, chewing gum, etc.

2 Raise your arms to 10 and 2 o'clock as if acknowledging applause.

3 Step forwards slightly with the left leg, your knee bent a little.

4 You can cartwheel left (left hand first) or right (right hand first), it's up to you.

5 Assuming you're going left, bend at the waist, reaching towards the ground with your left hand and kick your right leg into the air, up above your head.

6 Follow quickly with the right hand. As it touches the ground, your left leg should also have left the ground. Momentum and inertia provide the oomph as well as the stability in a cartwheel, so the slower you go, the less steady you will be. A good confident throw is what's needed to get you going.

7 Halfway through your cartwheel you will find yourself briefly in the straddle-handstand position. If you've tried a handstand, you'll know that it's hard to remain stable with legs pointing straight up. But it's easier in a cartwheel. With a bit of practice, a bit of speed, and *enough space* your legs should fly up.

8 Land with the right leg first, left leg next, finishing in the position you started, but with your right leg in front.

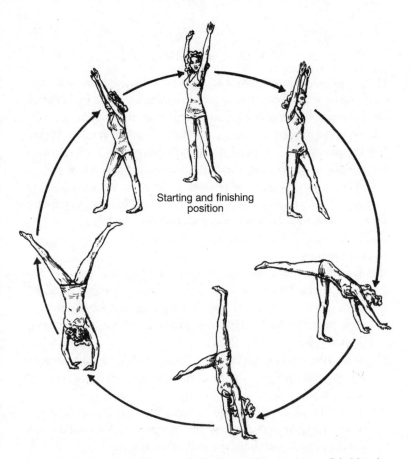

Starting and finishing
position

9   A good cartwheel requires rhythm and momentum. It's like the sails of Windy Miller's windmill: try thinking *hand, hand, foot, foot* as you go, moving in a straight line as if doing the cartwheel on a narrow bench. Try to keep your body *straight*. Most beginners do bent cartwheels but practice helps cure this fault.

10 No need to rush, but don't be hesitant either: you've really got to *go for it.*

❁ *The Cartwheel Galaxy is 500 million light-years from earth.* ❁

Curling for Beginners

Curlers have gone completely out of fashion. I remember in wartime films how every northern housewife used to wear them in her hair as she swilled the flags of a Saturday morning. I guess the passion-killing element did for them in the end. Of course, 'curlers' is also a word that describes those wacky people who curl. Curling is certainly a wonderful old sport; it began in 16th-century Scotland, where kilted highlanders with time on their hands whizzed stones called 'loafies' across the frozen lochs.

Today the game is played by teams of four in professional indoor arenas, using highly polished 3-stone (that's the *weight*) granite rocks and funny ice-brooms. The field (sheet) is marked out on the ice and is some 150 x 14ft in area. The ice is prepared by having water droplets sprayed onto its surface and the consequent bumps are called 'pebble' which, because of friction, cause the stone to turn in its path.

The object of the game is to slide the stone so that it stops at the far end of the sheet as close as possible to the centre of a 12ft-diameter bulls-eye called the 'house' (*see* illustration). The opposition then tries to knock the first team's stones away from the target and occupy the space with their own – a sort of ice pétanque. The stones must land between the *hog line* (where you start) and the *back line* (behind the rings), and between the boards or out lines (the sides). Teams play alternately until each has thrown eight stones: two per player. The score is then worked out. Is this making *any sense*?

TEAMS

The names of the players are based on the order in which they throw. The lead usually plays first, then the second, then the third, and finally the skip. But not always, just to make things confusing.

* *Lead*: the lead, or first, throws the team's first two stones, and sweeps for the others.

* *Second*: the second throws the third and fourth stones and also sweeps for other players.
* *Third*: the third is the deputy, also called the mate. She throws the team's fifth and sixth stones, and usually sweeps for the second and the lead. She plays before the skip and holds her brush for the skip to aim at. The thirds are also responsible for working out the score between themselves.
* *Skip*: the skip is captain and plays the last two stones which can often be decisive. She must therefore be the best player in the team. She holds the broom indicating where the other players must aim, but rarely does any sweeping. Typical!

So to recap: the lead throws first and second; the second third and fourth; the third fifth and sixth and the skip last. I hope that's clear.

Equipment
* *Stones*: specialist item not available from WH Smith. Try an iron in an emergency.
* *Brushes*: hog hair is most pleasing but synthetic materials are preferable because they don't moult on the ice.
* *Shoes*: a 'slippy' shoe on the left and a 'sticky' shoe on the right. *Honestly*, I'm not making this up.
* *Apparel*: dress warm, not in your bikini.

Play
Curling is always preceded by a handshake and the salutation: 'Good curling!' Fair enough, I suppose.

1 Stand with the stone in your right hand, weight on your left foot (slippy sole) and right leg behind you. With your brush extended to your left, which helps you balance, deliver your stone by sliding it from the hack: the push-off plate.
2 Aim at the brush held by the skip and as you let go give the stone a slight twist, which will cause it to bend its path. This is *not* why

the game is called curling. It comes from a Scots word meaning to rumble – get the idea?

3 If the skip says so, anyone not doing anything follows your stone up the ice with her broom, sweeping *in front of it* like a goodun. This reduces friction, making it go faster, further and straighter.

4 When all 16 shots are played, the thirds decide who wins, and by how much. Every stone beating an opponent's is awarded one 'shot'. This concludes one 'end'. A standard game lasts for eight or 10 ends.

5 There are many different shots allowed: stone budgers, bent ones and everything, and the glossary is huge. Where they get the time beats me.

Or you could have a glass of something and watch a Doris Day film.

❀ *You can walk for as far as 2 miles during an 8-end match.* ❀

How to
Throw Overarm

The plangently named Rachel Hayhoe Fint, former captain of the women's England cricket team, once said: 'I have nothing against man cricketers; some of them are quite nice people.' She went on, though, to describe professional cricket-coaching as, 'a man trying to get you to keep your legs together when other men have spent a lifetime trying to get them apart'. This showed, I think, that she was a woman of the world.

There are not, let's be honest, many successful women cricketers in England. If it comes to that, the men could do with a bit of practice too, judging by some of their dire performances of recent times. So I thought a little elementary instruction in the mechanics of the essential overarm technique might be useful for girls – using a *proper* cricket ball. There's only so much kudos to be secured by throwing underarm, and a tennis ball just adds an air of feebleness to the whole business.

When I showed this to my brother Tom, he said: 'It's not "throwing" Bunty, it's "*bowling*".' I had to explain to him that most girls have trouble enough *throwing* and I didn't want to discourage them by blinding them with science. Hence the title. Like everything else in the book, these instructions are for right-handers. If you're a left-hander, just reverse them. Anyway, here we go.

REQUIRED
* *A proper hard cricket ball*
* *White clothes, including trousers*
* *A set of stumps*
* *Someone to throw at*

INSTRUCTIONS
1   Stand sideways-on to your target (the lady at the other end with the cricket bat and the stumps), your left side facing the direction

in which you will toss the ball. (Or in which you *hope* to toss the ball.) We are omitting the run-up for the time being. I mean, be realistic.

2   Hold the ball in your right hand. The easy bit.

3   Polish it on your trousers. I haven't got a clue what this is supposed to do but it looks professional. *Note*: I now learn from my brother that polishing one side of the ball will affect the way it travels through the air ('spin'). It goes faster on the shiny side – but I don't think you should worry too much about this now.

4   Bring the ball up to your right jaw, sort of shot putterish. This is a preparatory position.

5   Using your outstretched left arm, point at the target (most often the stumps or bat).

6   Lean your weight back on to your right leg and allow the right arm to drop towards your bum.

THE RUNNING OVERARM THROW

7   Now transfer your weight forward on to the left leg, extending your right arm up from buttocks to ear, as you do, like the sweep of a windmill.

8   Your shoulders will rotate – the left moving backwards, right forwards, and as your right hand reaches 12 o'clock, you should snap your wrist forwards, releasing the ball at the apex.

9   Bring your hand forward and down in the follow-through.

10   Tea.

During the early stages of practice you will find that the ball occasionally flies out where you don't mean it to go. Your receiving batswoman should be encouraged, therefore, to wear helmet, pads and a cricketer's 'box', or what Rachel Hayhoe Flint used to call a 'manhole cover'.

❀ *Cricket is the second most popular sport in the world (soccer's first).* ❀

How to
Get Off a Ski Lift

*J*ust to remind you what a ski lift looks like, it's a sort of bench that sits in a sort of hoop attached to a sort of slowly-moving overhead contraption sort of thing. Its purpose is to take you effortlessly to the top of the slope – uphill skiing being an unrewarding pastime. Getting yourself on to one of these hummers is nuisance enough but getting off can be a horribly nerve racking enterprise – especially first time round. If you don't jump off quickly enough and get away from the article, it can actually pick you up again and take you all the way back down the mountain; don't laugh, I've seen it happen. So, screw up your courage and hold on to your elastic; here's the way to do it.

INSTRUCTIONS

1   In preparation for disembarking, put on your hat, gloves and goggles and securely pocket loose items: wintergreen lip balm, purse, reading glasses, small flasks of Schnapps.

2 Grab hold of a ski stick with each hand, but don't put on the wrist straps.

3 Always choose an edge seat if you can and avoid sitting next to a snowboarder; they can interfere with your skis.

4 Put your sticks under your outside leg. Be polite and point the spiky ends towards the edge of the chair, away from the person beside you. If you find yourself between two people, squeeze them tightly between your knees (the *sticks*) or hold the tips vertically with your hand at chest height so that they don't snag in the pile of snow at the top of the lift.

5 Point your ski-tips delicately upwards so that they don't catch the snow as you approach the getting-off point. If they do, you can find yourself suddenly and unceremoniously twisted about like a falling stand of snooker cues. Embarrassing. You might as well have a sign on your back saying: 'I don't have the first idea what I'm doing.'

6 As you approach the lift station, check the area for obstructions such as bags, St Bernards and unconscious lift casualties. Don't stick your legs out stiff and terrified or you'll snap them off like bread sticks when you reach the end. Relax them, in readiness for the smooth push-off.

7 Give yourself time to get hold of your sticks and prepare yourself for launch. When your chair has passed over the hillock, stand up and push off gently. Don't push too hard because the chair is about to turn and can swing about in ways that are difficult to predict.

8 Be aware that people will choose this moment to step on the backs of your skis, so keep your wits about you or you'll be falling over again.

9 Don't stop in front of the lift. Slither away into a safe zone, in as unhurried and unhumiliating a way as you can.

10 Rejoice at your safe deliverance and get some Schnapps inside you.

❈ *A 15-inch-wide snowflake fell on Montana in January 1887.* ❈

Horse Sense I
How to Identify the Parts of a Horse

When it comes to identifying the parts of a horse, I presume we can all manage the head, ears, hoof and tail. But what is the name for that bit right on the top of his head, between the ears? And where are the withers? And what is the gaskin? Well, one look at the 'horse map' below will turn you into an instant authority.

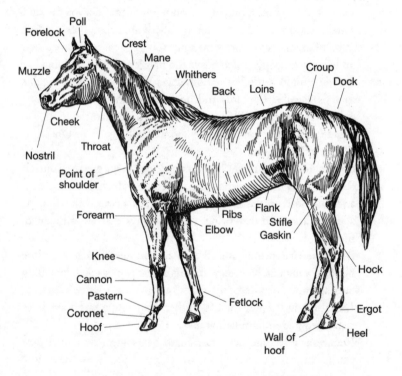

❀ *Camargue horses are born black but turn white as adults.* ❀

Horse Sense II
How to Groom a Horse

*M*ost of us, I suppose, go through a horsey phase when we are young. I had posters of ponies on my wall at home but took them down when I became more interested in the lads at the stables, after a toothy gelding picked me up by the hair. Some of us, though, never grow out of the horsey phase.

Grooming, is something you can do even if you only ever fall off horses; it is good isometric and spiritual exercise for the horse, and for you too. So here's a guide to the basics.

REQUIRED

* *A curry-comb: an oval rubber-tooth brush*
* *A dandy brush: a stiff-bristle brush*
* *A body brush: a soft-bristle brush*
* *A plastic mane comb (plastic comb, not plastic mane)*
* *A towel or rag*

INSTRUCTIONS

1 First tie your horse safely, then groom him from neck to tail, doing the starboard (right) and port (left) flanks in turn.

2 Begin by using the curry-comb in a circular motion to loosen and bring to the surface dirt and dust that have settled under the hair. While you work, the comb will release natural oils, giving your horse's coat a healthy lustre. Take care of the bony bits though – back and shoulders in particular, and don't use a curry-comb on the legs. Never do his face this way; it's far too rough and you might cause eye injuries.

3 Once you've finished with the curry-comb, use the stiff dandy brush to 'flick' the coat up so that the dirt comes away in light clouds. It's rather like a floor-brush action: flick, flick, flick.

4 When you have given the horse a thorough going over with the

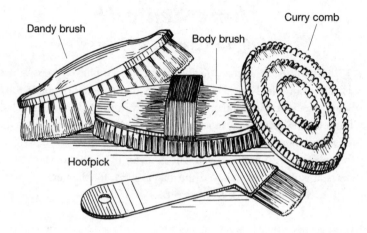

dandy brush, smooth down his hair with the soft-bristle body brush and sweep away final traces of mud and dust. The body brush stroke is quite unlike that of the dandy brush. Smooth the coat down flat in the direction of hair growth. This should produce an immaculate burnished appearance.

5   Now gently run the comb through the horse's mane. Like the tail, the mane can be delicate, so a plastic brush is best. If you want to plait the mane *see* opposite for full instructions.

6   Use the dandy brush for the tail. Be careful, though, because the tail hairs can break easily. Don't brush vigorously and don't use a comb.

7   Finally, use a plain towel or rag to wipe over the horse's coat. This will bring up a luminous gleam. My Uncle Vivian always finished with a sheen-enhancing conditioner. But he used to polish his horse to such a brilliantly high gloss that riding became hazardous and he was always slipping off like a penguin on an eminence.

❀ *The longest recorded mane was 18ft. It was grown by a mare called Maude.* ❀

Horse Sense III
How to Plait a Horse's Mane

*T*he 'pastern' is the bit of the equine leg between the ergot and hoof, but in his dictionary Dr Johnson defined it as, 'the *knee* of a horse'. When a pestilential woman asked why he'd got it wrong, he replied, 'Ignorance, Madam, ignorance,' which was both witty and honest. By the way, if like me you thought that ergot was just a cereal fungus, then you might like to peruse the excellent 'horse map' on page 174, where you'll discover all the bits of a horse helpfully labelled.

To plait good plaits, you'll need a mane that is not too ragged and a horse who will stand still. It can be a fiddlesome business, so it is a good idea to wear a cotton stockman's coat or failing that an old quilted dressing gown so you can keep your scissors and thread in the pockets while you're working. Should your horse be fidgety, you can smooth things along by threading a separate needle for each plait, and pinning them down the front. Take care not to break the hairs.

REQUIRED
* *A plastic mane comb*
* *A water brush (specialist horsey item)*
* *A pair of scissors with round ends*
* *Blunt darning needle/s with a large eye*
* *Some cotton thread, matching the mane*
* *A bag of rubber bands*

INSTRUCTIONS
1 First follow the grooming instructions on page 175–6.
2 Using your fingers and the mane comb, divide the mane hair into equal clumps, and put a rubber band around each.
3 Starting at the poll (*see* horse map), dampen each clump of hair with a water brush and lay it flat. These articles resemble the

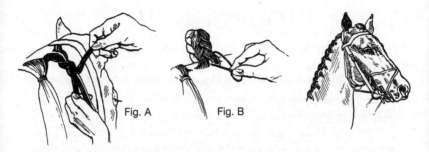

Fig. A   Fig. B

scrubbing brushes that the housewife of yesteryear used to swill the flags and are gettable from horsey suppliers.

4   Tie an 18in length of thread to the eye of the needle so it won't come off and get lost in the mane or on the ground if you drop it.

5   Start plaiting from the ear-end (I'm assuming you know how to plait, if not see pages 115–117), weaving the thread tidily into the plait as you go (Fig. A).

6   Plait as far as you can, then wrap the thread around the tuft and tie off with a half-hitch (look, you'll just have to ask a sailor or look it up on the internet or something; *I can't do everything*).

7   Pass the needle through the root of the mane, folding the plait in half and in half again.

8   Stick the needle back through the folded plait and the root and tie off by stitching through the plait a couple of times (Fig. B).

9   Finish by plaiting the forelock.

❈ *Dr Johnson suffered from twitches and tics.* ❈

How to
Make a Garden in a Bottle

Should you live in a flat or have little time for tending a large garden, why not start a dwarf garden in a glass bottle or demijohn? The bottle garden is a self-sufficient world which you can cultivate open or closed. Unlike the open variety, the lidded bottle garden retains moisture, and generally makes more of a demand on your time. The open garden is easier, and its plants will often grow up and out of the bottle, and hang attractively down the outside.

Open or closed, bottle gardening can become an absorbing interest, and a great relief from the strains of modern life. You are Queen of this miniature universe and there is nothing nicer than to sit on a summer's evening and just watch your developing biosphere.

REQUIRED

* *A wide necked decorative glass bottle, big enough to get your hand into*
* *Some ordinary houseplant compost*
* *A bag of fine alpine gravel, or similar (ask the advice of the nice man at the garden centre)*
* *A few miniature plants: anything decorative will do that won't grow too big and that can stand the moist environment*
* *For the ambitious, some long thin gardening tools (you might have to improvise)*

THE OPEN GARDEN

An open bottle garden, containing ground plants and maybe a few small animals such as earthworms, is suited to those with a flair for the architecture of small spaces but without the luxury of endless time.

INSTRUCTIONS

1   Line the bottom of your bottle with about 2ins of gravel, to create drainage.
2   Evenly spread 2–3ins of compost on top.
3   Plant your dwarf plants into the soil, spreading them around evenly. Even in a large bottle four or five plants will be plenty. Put the taller ones at the back or in the middle, and the shorter ones in front or round the outside.
4   Sprinkle a little more gravel on top of the compost. This acts as a mulch, preventing dehydration and also sets off your plants attractively.

5   Keep your bottle garden in a light position and water regularly. Be cautious however, making sure you don't inundate the soil. A cupful three times a week is about right, depending on the ambient temperature, and the season.

6   Replant your bottle garden twice a year so as to inhibit disease, and to allow for the growth of your mini plants. Carefully pull them out and put them into little pots with some fertilizer. Clean out the bottle thoroughly and replace your plants with new specimens. Tidy up the gravel surface.

There is no need to feed the plants in your bottle garden; there is enough nourishment in the compost to keep them going for their lifetime in the jar.

THE SEALED GARDEN

The sealed garden is best if you have a bit more time to spare and are prepared to create what is effectively a self-sustaining ecosystem. You will have to use the right sort of plants and take the time to find a few suitable animals to keep the thing going.

INSTRUCTIONS

The method is much the same as that for the open garden. Your sealed environment needs moist soil, a few plants, and some little animals like terrestrial isopods: worms, woodlice and other small segmented creatures are the ones to look out for.

Your plants must be small and resistant to high levels of moisture – rotten roots is a common problem with a sealed garden – and they must be slow growers.

A sealed garden is happiest in a cool bright situation, *away from direct sunlight* so that Willy Worm and Wendy Woodlouse don't fry under the glass.

❀ *'Bonsai' means 'tray planting' in Japanese.* ❀

How to
Make a Snow Angel

*T*his climate change business is a bit of a pest, what with palm trees growing on Mount Everest, sharks swimming round Iceland and local schoolchildren making snowmen out of nothing but rain.

But every now and again it does still snow. In fact, the mere dusting of half an inch can close schools and factories, stop trains and bring everything south of Aberdeen to a grinding halt. So when it snows, it's time to gird your loins, don your warmest kit and make snow angels. What do you mean, you've never made a snow angel? Put on your mittens at once and let's get out there.

You make one by lying on your back and sweeping your arms and legs through the snow so that the heavenly being's wings and celestial habit are described on the ground.

INSTRUCTIONS

1 Dress warm, including hat and gloves.

2 Go out and find a pristine area of frosty or powdery snow. Wet snow doesn't work so well.

3 Fall gently backwards and lie flat, arms by your side. (You should have previously checked for barely concealed jagged rocks and tent pegs.)

4 Now sweep your arms straight up so they touch your ears. Then sweep them down till they touch your sides again. Repeat the action a few times; you are making the wings.

5 Next, sweep your legs apart as far as they will go, and then together again. You're now creating the angelic habiliment.

6 Here's the tricky bit: get up without destroying your handiwork. A trail of boot marks and handprints all over your angel's holy garb spoils the aesthetics. A good way to get up neatly is to extend your arms and ask a friend at your feet to pull you up.

7 Survey the picture you've made. It doesn't half look like an angel.

8 Take a picture with your mobile and send it to everyone.

9 Go back inside for a mug of mulled wine and a biscuit.

❀ *Angels feature in Christianity, Islam, Judaism and Zoroastrianism.* ❀

Pet Care: How to Worm a Cat

When I began looking into this topic I was convinced that it ought to be possible to give a cat a worming pill without dragging the emaciated creature all the way down to the vet's in one of those 'baskets'. Just as I was thinking that getting a cat *into* one of those baskets deserved a page to itself, I stumbled on an old document in my files that sets out in blunt terms the stark difficulty of the whole enterprise. The haunting quality of these instructions seemed truer to life than the bald directions on my packet of Wormola so I have written them down for you under the *real world* heading below. May God have mercy on your soul.

How to give a cat a pill in an ideal world

1   Hold cat's head firmly and open mouth.
2   Put pill at back of throat.
3   Hold mouth shut and massage throat until cat swallows pill.

If cat spits out pill

1   Hide pill in lump of cheese.
2   Give cat pill in smoked fish to disguise horrid taste.
3   Coat in Marmite or Bovril (pill, not cat).
4   If cat just licks Marmite off pill, crumble up and sprinkle on food.

How to give a cat a pill in the real world

1   Cradle cat in crook of left arm, place right forefinger and thumb either side of cat's mouth and gently squeeze cheeks. Pop pill into mouth and let cat swallow.
2   Retrieve pill from under TV and cat from behind sofa. Repeat step 1.
3   Recover cat from bedroom and discard sodden pill. Pop out new pill from fancy foil dispenser. Cradle cat in left arm holding rear paws tightly with left hand. Force jaws open and push pill to back of throat with right forefinger. Hold mouth shut for a count of 10.
4   Bathe bites with soothing unguent, rescue pill from under book-shelf and cat from top of wardrobe. Call man from garden. Kneel on floor, with cat tightly between knees. Grip front and rear paws, ignoring weird primaeval growling from cat. Get man to grip head firmly with one hand and force ruler into cat's mouth. Roll pill down ruler into mouth and massage cat's throat like pâté de foie gras goose.
5   Tear cat from expensive curtain, get another pill and sweep shattered Spode and family heirloom figurines into wastepaper basket. Run scratched arms under cold tap.
6   Wrap cat in a large bath towel, head just visible. Ask man to lie on cat and put pill into end of drinking straw. Force cat's mouth open with pencil and blow pill down cat's throat.

7   Check label to see if harmful to humans. Gargle with Scotch to take away taste, while sponging worst of blood from carpet.

8   Drag cat from behind washing machine and put in cupboard, closing door on cat's neck, but leave head showing. Force mouth open with a large spoon. Flick pill down throat with rubber band.

9   Apply ice pack to rubber-band-shape welt on cheek, and find pill.

10   Call fire brigade to get cat down from top of poplar tree.

11   Tie cat's front and rear paws with twine, like suckling pig. Bind to table leg. Don heavy-duty pruning gauntlets and motorbike helmet. Push pill into mouth followed by large piece of steak. Holding head vertically, pour two pints of water into cat's throat to wash down.

12   Open bottle of industrial strength vodka. Bathe wounds with half and drink rest.

To give a dog a pill: wrap it in bacon.

❀ *Cat bites are rarer than dog bites but more prone to infection.* ❀

How to
Play Hopscotch

*T*here was this girl I remember at school called Gloria Oppenheimer, which was as good a name as anyone could ask for. She manifested the earliest and most magnificent mammarial exhibition of any of us, and, because of her initials (I *think*), she was known to every one as 'Go!'

Anyway, years passed – as they say in books – and she became a simultaneous translator at the UN. Then one day she bumped into a man on the stairs in San Diego and ended up as an actor/director in/of – how shall I put it? – exotic films. She deserves a book all to herself, does Gloria. The thing was, though, that she had this phenomenal memory and knew more skipping and hopscotch songs than any of us.

There was the delightful (now politically out of favour):

My mother said
I never should
Play with the Gypsies in the wood.
If I did
She would say,
'Naughty girl to disobey'.

This scanned and rhymed but there was also a charmless lumpen one with technical problems, especially in line 2, that Gloria used to chant before throwing her stone:

I've got my favourite pebble,
I'm going to get to go.
I'm a hopscotch lover
It's my turn to throw.

Anyway, to come to the point, here are the rules of hopscotch.

THE GAME

Known all over the world, hopscotch began in Roman Britain when soldiers were made to run 100ft-long military hopscotch courts in full kit. The name is a mixture of 'hop' meaning to hop (obviously) and 'escocher', a French word meaning to cut. No, I wasn't any the wiser either. In Germany they call it *templehupfen*, and *hinkelbaan* in the Low Countries. Which serves them right.

Each player has her own pebble or small stone, which marks her position throughout the game. The idea is to chase the stone through a chalk-drawn grid, with a mixture of hops and jumps. These grids vary slightly from country to country and even locally. The one in the illustration is fairly typical and resembles those we used at school. You mustn't touch the lines with your stone or foot, or put down your hand to balance. The game is, therefore, a mixture of chess, Twister and sumo. The winner is the first girl to complete the course the requisite number of times.

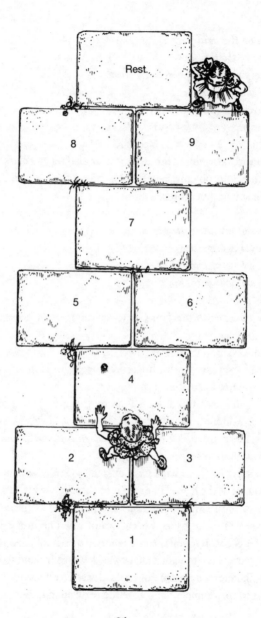

PLAYING

1 Draw the grid and its numbers with a piece of chalk (*see* illustration). My school was on a chalk cliff and lumps of the stuff were everywhere in the flowerbeds. We used them as stones, and for drawing the court too.

2 Do an *ip-dip* to decide who goes first.

3 Assuming you are first to go, start by throwing your stone into box 1. The aim is to get it to land in that box. If it does, you can begin the hopping business. This takes a bit of explaining. You may have only one foot in any numbered square. So you must balance on one leg in single numbered squares but may straddle double squares, alternating your landing foot as you go. When you reach the 'home' or 'rest' square at the top you may land any way you wish. When ready, jump around and return, picking up your stone on the way. If it's in box 1 pick it up when your feet are in boxes 2/3. If successful you may now go on to square 2 and so on. If you foul by throwing the stone out of the intended box, land on a line, overbalance, miss a square, or forget to collect your stone, play passes to the next girl. Sometimes the rule is that any box containing a stone must be missed. Things can get quite exciting if there are more than three players.

I wonder what Gloria is up to these days.

❀ *Chalk is formed underwater from the bodies of marine organisms.* ❀

How to
Play Jacks

When my brother was a boy and I was a girl he played conkers and I played jacks. That was the law. My friend Lucy was an expert then, and could play for hours. Now she lectures in dentistry and continues to play a mean game, using a set of polyurethane display teeth.

Jacks, sometimes called jackstones or onesies, is hundreds of years old, just like conkers, and is based on the ancient game of fivestones that was played with five small pebbles, or sheep's knucklebones, in the days before My Little Pony and DVDs.

EQUIPMENT

Apart from the small rubber ball (usually terracotta coloured), a set of jacks consists of between five and 15 small, metal 'asters', each consisting of a four-pointed cross, with 'blobs' at its tips, positioned centrally, about a blobless spin-able axis. The playing field is almost always the tarmac of a playground, but the game works on a wood floor too or any other hard surface. The boundary is informal, and is roughly an arm's length from the two players.

THE 'PLAIN-GAME'

After an *ip-dip* to decide who goes first, the jacks are scattered on the ground. The competitors then take turns to play. One turn involves picking up the jacks (after a formula: *see* below), while bouncing and catching the ball. *Usually.* Of course you may already be shaking your head because you played it some other way. Indeed, just like conkers, the regional variations are many, and even in a single town there might be 10 or 15 different versions of the game, involving changes to the number of bounces, hands in use, number of jacks to be picked up in one go, and so on. Occasionally the ball is bounced straight off the ground, or sometimes no bounce is allowed, just the upwards throw (*tricky*). There may even be penalties for fouls such as accidentally nudging a jack that you are not picking up. These are often of the miss-a-go type. In some games you are allowed to separate two contiguous jacks by calling 'kissing cousins!' or 'snog-buster!' while parting them with a finger-poke. Game variations go by exotic names such as double-bounce, eggs in the basket and round the world.

Generally an escalating sequence of pick-ups is the rule, starting with one (onesies) and moving up to fivesies – or more if you have more jacks. Fewer jacks (usually five) are used in the UK than in the US variety of the game where a dozen or 15 can be the rule. In most versions one hand only may be employed for bounces and pick-ups, though the jacks are often put in, or on the back of, the redundant hand, as they are collected. The girl to progress furthest is the winner.

A WALK-THROUGH

This five-jacks variant of the game is called one-hand, one-bounce, granny, or plain-game jacks. Other versions ring the changes on this basic idea. Let's assume you've *ip-dipped* and are to go first.

1 Broadcast the jacks on the ground.
2 Throw the ball up with the right hand.
3 With the same hand pick up a jack (this is onesies), letting the ball bounce once.
4 Allow the ball to drop back into the right hand, which contains one jack.
5 Pass the jack to the left hand, retaining the ball in the right.
6 Now repeat with one more jack, continuing in the same way until all the jacks are collected. Twosies is the same as onesies, except now you must grab, hold and transfer two jacks at a time. *Note*: with each game after onesies, there will be a remainder of jacks smaller than the number you are supposed to pick up. Pick them up in the same way, nonetheless, at the last bounce.
7 As soon as you fail to pick up the jack/s or the correct number, or the ball bounces more than once or rolls away or you commit some other foul, your turn ends and your opponent takes over. If she messes up then the game comes back to you and you start again at the number you failed on first time around.

SPECIMEN FOULS
* Failing to catch the ball
* Dropping jacks or ball
* Picking up the wrong number of jacks
* Touching other jacks
* Catching the ball too early or too late
* Using both hands or the wrong hand

Please don't play with plastic 'safety' jacks; they are so light that they are almost impossible to pick up. They normally come with a monstrously unbouncy sinister plastic ball. These rubbishy space-age jacks are for dilettantes, amateurs and Sunday players only.

❈ *The name 'Jack' is from Jankin, a medieval diminutive of 'John' (Hebrew).* ❈

How to
Read the Tealeaves

*T*he teabag is a modern miracle of convenience but it has pretty much done for the art of tasseography or tealeaf reading, though some practitioners are still to be found. Romance, health, work and money are the life-zones on which tasseographers tend to concentrate their focus and tealeaf reading is the perfect diversion for any girl with eyes good enough to see the bottom of the vicar's teacup – whether for fun or profit. But you must use real loose tea; there's only so much predictive insight you can squeeze out of a cold teabag. Here are the basics.

INSTRUCTIONS

Take a cup containing tea dregs and vigorously swirl the detritus three times in a clockwise direction, allowing the tealeaves to slosh up and around the sides of the cup. When they have come to rest, peer sagaciously into the interior. It helps to wear big earrings.

The tealeaves should have settled in 'swarms' on the cup's inner surface. These shapes are the symbols that you will read and you should begin by looking for the simplest figures. The following forms have traditionally been associated with portent of different kinds.

* Triangles: a sign of good karma
* Circles: betoken success
* Squares: indicate the need for caution

It's a bit like the road signs in the *Highway Code*.

You will probably also see letters – which refer to the names of friends or relations – numbers (connoting time) and, frequently, human faces – smiles and frowns. Most of the shapes may look like nothing much at first, but the harder you peer the more likely they are to assume meaningful form: a tree, a horse, a serpent, Gyles Brandreth. Symbols near the rim are important, life-changing omens. Those on the sides of the cup are significant, but not earth-shattering. Figures on the bottom indicate change. Here are a few of the easiest to read, along with a guide to their interpretation.

Acorn: at the top – success; at the bottom – robust health

Anchor: rest, stability, constancy

Arrow: bad love news

Bell: unexpected news – good if near the top

Cabbage: jealousy; if speckled – jealousy at work

Cigar: new friends

Dish: trouble at home

Duck: money on the way

Elephant: wisdom and strength

Fan: romance

Fork: false flattery

Harp: love

Horn: prodigality

Horse's head: a lover

Insect: petty problems

Kangaroo: domestic harmony

Lamp: at the top – a banquet; on the side – secrets revealed

Man: near handle – a visitor

Mushroom: at the top – a move to the country

Octopus: danger

Ostrich: travel

Parasol: a new lover

Raven: bad news

Ring: at the top – an offer of marriage; if broken – broken engagement

Scissors: quarrels

Spider: work success

Thimble: change at home

Umbrella: aggravation

Vase: a friend in need

Wasp: stalled romance

Xylophone: I made that one up. Nobody's ever seen a xylophone in the leaves

Zebra: overseas adventure

Sometimes it's hard to tell an octopus (danger) from a spider (work success) or a raven (bad news) from a duck (money on the way). I'm sorry, you're on your own here.

THE WHEN

Your subject's teacup is like a clock. Its handle, held at 9 o'clock, represents now, the time and place of the reading, with each quarter-hour standing for a three-month period. For example, any shapes at 12 o'clock, indicate happenings three months into the future, anything at 3 o'clock is six months down the road, and swirls at 6 o'clock, represent doings in your subject's life nine months hence. By going round clockwise you can predict forthcoming happenings as much as a year into the future, and by subdividing the quarters you can make predictions for periods shorter than three months. But anything under a month is touch and go.

More tea, Vicar?

❀ *A zarf is an ornamental holder for a handle-less cup.* ❀

How to
Water Ski

*D*uring the summer of 1922, in what must be *the* sports brainwave of the twentieth century, 18-year-old Ralph Samuelson of Lake City, Minnesota decided there was no reason why the principles of skiing on snow could not be applied to water.

And so it was that on June 28, with two barrel staves under his feet and being towed across the Mississippi River by his brother Ben, Ralph Samuelson majestically failed to water ski, being instead dragged several yards before plunging impressively under the river surface.

Like all obsessives, however, he kept on going, replacing the barrel slats with a pair of proper snow skis. Now, swept along behind a motor boat powered by an enormous converted truck engine, he began to sniff the sweet smell of success, managing to stay on top of the water.

Within days Ralph had invested in some leather straps and was refining his technique by leaning backwards as he was whisked along, his ski tips slanted cheerfully upwards. From then on it was clear his new technique would take off, and today water skiing has become a glamorous sport beloved of svelte ladies and gentlemen in figure-hugging costumes, who zoom gracefully all over places like Lake Geneva.

SAFETY FIRST

Remember *it takes three to ski*: one to drive the boat, one to do the skiing (you), and one to do nothing but watch you from the boat (the spotter); *very important* that. The guy driving the boat is in charge of your safety so have a proper discussion beforehand to set out some rules. Plan where the boat will go and make sure everyone knows who is responsible for what. A tranquil surface is important too. Waves are your enemy.

Other obvious safety matters include not doing it if you can't swim, getting a pro to take you through your first few attempts, not trying it in the public swimming baths and so on. You'll also improve safety if you use decent equipment. It's no good tying two ironing boards to your feet and hoping for the best.

TOP 10 TIPS

1   Wear a life jacket designed for water skiing and tighten the straps, which can whip you in the wind.
2   Remove all jewellery.
3   Use a tow rope at least 75ft long.
4   Never wrap any part of the line around your body.
5   Keep away from the propeller. Always.
6   Have a spotter on board to take your signals and tell the driver if you fall.
7   Go over the hand signals before you get in the water.
8   Know the area. Your driver should avoid the shallows and the submerged shopping trolleys, but be aware of potential hazards yourself.

9   Pay attention to what other boaters are doing and give them a wide berth.
10 Don't ski in the dark or if you've been drinking. *Obviously.*

EIGHT SAFETY SIGNALS

1   Thumb up = *speed up*
2   Thumb down = *slow down*
3   Flat hand = *stop*
4   Cut throat = *I want to let go the rope*
5   Finger point left and finger point right = *turn the boat in direction indicated*
6   Pat your head = *I want to return to the boat*
7   Make circle of thumb and forefinger = *OK* or *signal understood*
8   Hands clasped over head = *I'm OK* (after falling)

GET GOING

There's nothing complicated about any of this but it does require some practice, with guidance from a good instructor.

1   Get in the water and move well away from the boat before the engine is started.
2   Signal once you're ready to go.
3   As the boat slowly moves forward the line will tighten. When you give a thumb's up the boat will move off in a straight line with enough thrust to lift you up out of the water. Lean back and once you are up, signal to your spotter so that the boat's speed can be adjusted to your requirements. Then hang on and get the feel of things. You will fall over a lot; don't worry about it.
4   If (*when*) you fall, give the OK sign as soon as you safely can to let the crew know you are uninjured, so you can be picked up and get going again.
5   When you've fallen, hold a ski out of the water while you wait to be recovered. This makes you very visible to other craft.

6   The boat will come back and circle you slowly either to give you back the tow line or pick you up if you've had enough.

7   Wait for the engine to be switched off before you get aboard.

A FINAL WORD OF WARNING

The Newtonian forces at work while you water ski are pretty powerful and must be taken into account when you choose your bathing suit. It should be tight, robust and very clingy round your bum. This is not vanity but self-preservation. My dear friend Veronica told me – and her story was backed up by the experiences of my good friend Helen – that she now always wears a wetsuit when water skiing. This change of attire followed a startling experience after she fell when water skiing in Canada. She told me she found herself being dragged along at speed – bum first – and that the force of the incoming water was such that she was made the victim of an instantaneous, powerful and unasked-for colonic irrigation. With friends like that, who needs enemas?

❀ *Lake Geneva is the second largest freshwater lake in Central Europe.* ❀

How to
Be the Perfect Cheerleader

When she was at college my American sister-in-law used to be a cheerleader. She told me it was jolly hard work getting all the girls to bounce up and down in time with each other, while smiling the rictus-cheerleader-smile and singing the jolly cheerleader song:

We must, we must,
We must increase our bust!
The bigger, the better,
The tighter the sweater;
The boys depend on us!

This doggerel struck me as typically American in its up-frontness but I'm not sure it would have much impressed feminist Andrea Dworkin. My Uncle Bob, however, has certainly been affected by the emotion of it and has taken to singing it himself down the pub, doing a version of the pom-pom actions – a cushion in each hand. The wry amusement of his associates is reflected in the thoughtful pleasantries they call out as he boings up and down in the snug.

Being a cheerleader requires a diverse range of skills, not least of which are stamina, good aerobic capacity and robust cardiovascular health. A loud voice with plangent, distance-covering qualities is also desirable, along with a pair of strong legs. The list below gives you a few more tips.

* Smear a good inch of fake tan all over before donning your lurid 'spankies' or 'lollipops' (briefs). Those floodlights will otherwise wash all the colour out of you.
* Long curly hair that jounces prettily is the best. Think 70s Olivia Newton-John and get hold of some curling tongs.
* Bright vermilion mouth-emphasizing lipstick is a must, as is a good thick black eyebrow pencil and heavy mascara. You are fighting the lights, don't forget.
* I haven't space here to go into the moves in detail – just follow the other girls. Many of the actions are derived from the jumping-up-and-down school of dance, and are designed to accentuate your femininity in a way that will be noticeable by the crowd from where they are sitting. I don't wish to put it any more bluntly than that.
* Drink plenty of water.
* Smile, even when you are hot, tired and want to go home.

TO MAKE YOUR OWN POM-POMS

1 Cut two ring doughnut-shaped circles of cardboard about 1ft across.
2 Superimpose them and evenly wind several yards of scenes-of-crime tape around the doughnut, tying the end of one

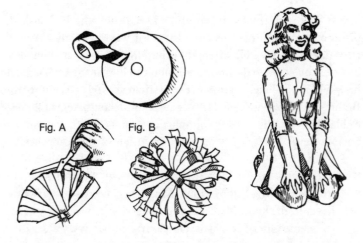

Fig. A   Fig. B

piece on to the next until you have a thickish layer.

3   Pass one blade of a pair of very sharp scissors between the cardboard doughnuts (through the tape), and slice right around the circumference, cutting through the tapes (Fig. A).

4   Tie a length of tape tightly round the middle, between the cardboard rings (Fig. B).

5   Snip the cardboard circles and remove, shaking out the finished pom-pom.

6   Add a handle.

❀ *Cheerleading started at Princeton University in the 1880s.* ❀

How to
Blag Your Way in Classical Music

*W*hen I was at school there were a number of music staff who managed to give us a bit of the history, a dollop of theory and plenty of practice, while making the whole subject seem delightful fun. I remember Mr George in particular. He was a short, white-haired Scot with stubby fingers and a tweed suit, who had pushed a piano over the Cairngorms and claimed it was this, rather than his 20-a-day Capstan Full Strength habit, that had given him heart disease. You could make up a tune, hum it to him at the keyboard and he would immediately harmonize it in whatever style you chose from Brahms to boogie-woogie. He was a *real* musician so he had no need to blag his way. But if you're not much of a music buff, you can *seem* terribly clever just by airily regurgitating a few of these key facts.

SOME USEFUL MUSIC BLAGGING FACTS AND FIGURES

* *The Middle Ages*: 400s–1500s. Music first begins to be written down in the 800s. Medieval monks develop 'plainsong', an unaccompanied liturgical chant. No electric guitars yet. Hildegard of Bingen, German monastic mystic and musician, writes oratorios for her nuns.

* *Late Medieval–Renaissance*: 1300–1600. The age of out-of-tuneness with croaky polyphonic harmony. Lizards, shawms, sackbutts, racketts, crumhorns, seven-foot-long trumpets marine and other wacky instruments accompany a lot of chicken legs being thrown over shoulders. The funniest instrument ever – the serpent: a cross between a huge black pudding, a vacuum cleaner and a saxophone – is invented in 1590 by Canon Edmé Guillaume in Auxerre, France. Loads of church music is produced, with Palestrina leading the field. Plenty of women composers too, including the snazzy-sounding Lucrezia Orsina Vizzana. The First opera – *Dafne* – composed by Jacopo Peri in 1597. Lutenist Bálint Bakfark 1507–1576 has a really good name.

* *Baroque*: 1600s. Music becomes curlier and cleverer. Britain can boast Henry Purcell, Lady Mary Dering and Giles Farnaby (a dab hand on the virginals), but two Germans, J S Bach and G F Handel, lead an international field. Then Herr Handel becomes a British subject and moves into number 25 Upper Brook Street as Mr Handel, next door to Jimi Hendrix, at number 23.

* *The Classical period*: 1750–1820. First symphonies appear. Some really good silly names too, including Florian Leopold Gassmann, August Carl Ditters von Dittersdorf and the exotic-sounding Anna Amalia, Duchess of Saxe-Weimar-Eisenach and Fanny Krumpholtz Pittar. A great deal of deeply boring music is churned out. A time of dumbing down really, but with some golden nuggets among the slag: Mozart, Schubert, Haydn, Beethoven. And women too, I'm delighted to say, including Maria Anna Walburga Ignatia 'Nannerl' Mozart: Wolfi's long-winded sister.

* *Romantic era*: 1820s–1910. Self-conscious emotionalism and the drama of story-telling. Ludwig Spohr, Franz Liszt and Frédéric Chopin are early Romantics and Tchaikovsky is typical of the late school, as is Master of the King's Musick, Edward Elgar in Britain. There's Mahler, *Richard* Strauss (not the Waltz man, a different chap) and loads of women again, including the super sounding Constance Faunt Le Roy Runcie. First photographs of musicians appear, as does Engelbert Humperdinck (1854–1921): not the chap with the microphone but the one with the high forehead and the fantastic curly moustache. Excellent!

* *The Modern era*: 1900s till now. Mood, atmosphere, self-consciousness and a calculated upsetting of the musical apple cart. Here are just some of them, in no particular order: Berg, Bartók, Britten, Boulez, Ives, Debussy, Stravinsky, Ravel, Prokofiev and loads more. And they're still at it, including the women, of whom my favourite for a good name is the terse Meredith Monk. She says: 'I work between the cracks.' Excellent Meredith. My favourite of the squeaky gate and broken glass school is Elliot Carter. I think he's really got something. Have a listen.

❈ *J S Bach had 20 children of whom 10 died in infancy.* ❈

How to
Forecast the Weather Like Your Grandma Used To

*D*o you remember Michael Fish who used to do the weather on the telly? He was famous for a number of things including his lively jackets, nerdy hair and Nostradamus-type meteorological prognostications such as, 'Clouds bubbling up along the east coast', and, 'So there'll be plenty of sunshine in time for Ascot', and, 'Earlier on today, apparently, a woman rang the BBC and said she'd heard there was a hurricane on the way. Well, if you're watching, don't worry, there isn't'. He said this immediately before the worst storm to hit south-east England for 290 years tore down six of Sevenoaks's seven oaks, hurled beach huts across roads, felled buildings and killed 19 people.

Weather forecasters often seem to have trouble with their premonitions, even with the help of computers, and I think we should go back to the old days when forecasts were done in verse. A red sky at night invariably meant delighted shepherds and if it was dry in Rye and cool in Goole, everyone in Lissingdown knew to take an umbrella.

My grandma used to hang seaweed outside her back door as a kind of weather teller. She told me she relied on it for her forecasts and knew that if the seaweed was dry the weather had been fair but if it was wet it had been raining. I realized quite early on that she was barking mad but liked her because of her fat arms, wooly pink cardy and the boxes of chocolates she always turned up with. She had a number of other 'weather tellers' about the house too, and this is how to make my favourite of them.

WEATHER-TELLING MR OSTRICH
Put a fir cone in a warm oven, removing it once it is dry enough that its scales open wide. It will now be highly sensitive to changes in

atmospheric moisture: when the air is dry, and the weather likely to be fine, the scales will open wide. If unsettled weather is on the way, the scales will be partly closed. When rain is coming, the cone will be tightly shut.

REQUIRED

* *A fir cone*
* *A 2in square of corrugated cardboard*
* *A piece of thick white card*
* *Pliable but stiffish fuse wire*
* *Pliers*
* *PVA glue or Plasticine*
* *A sharp craft knife*
* *Watercolour paints*

INSTRUCTIONS

1 Start by twisting together three pieces of pliable wire, opening them out at one end to form the feet.

2 Stick the feet to a square of corrugated card and allow to dry. This will allow you enough time to do your nails *and* have a cup of coffee.

3 Attach the feet to the body with some lumps of Plasticine (quicker) or PVA glue (stronger). Allow to dry.

4 Cut Mr Ostrich's neck and head from a piece of stiff card and, once decorated with a cheerful beaky smile and eyes, push the neck end into a slit in the base of the cone. Make the slit with a sharp knife but mind your fingers.

Mr Ostrich makes a fantastic present for children and is as reliable as Mr Fish.

❀ *Seaweeds are marine algae.* ❀

How to
Identify British Wild Flowers

William Blake wrote a poem called *The Wild Flower's Song* that goes: 'As I wander'd the forest, / The green leaves among, / I heard a wild flower / Singing a song.' He might just as well have written: 'As I wander'd the forest, / 'Mongst green leaves so hazy, / I saw a young choir boy / Who looked like a daisy.' It makes about as much sense. Moreover my second line isn't back-to-front like his is. I think I'll send it off to Hallmark.

Anyhow, I wanted to talk to you about our wild flowers. If you have a look at the illustrations these botanical notes should help you identify a few of our more interesting specimens.

1   The bluebell is really *the* British flower. I know roses are wonderful but this quintessentially woodland flower bursts forth in spring, carpeting huge areas of shaded forest and park in a uniquely British way. There's an old steam railway in Sussex called the Bluebell Railway and in the summer you can sit in a carriage amongst white high-class napery and white middle-class people and be served a delicious and expensive dinner with candles while the train chugs and hoots through the darkling countryside. No bluebells to be seen though, they've all withered and gone brown by then.

2   The poppy is unmissable by its pillarbox hue and hairy stalk. When I was a girl, poppies were few and far between but now they grow like weeds all along the roadside. Last year as I was driving over the South Downs I noticed a red square on the horizon; it was a wheat field overgrown with poppies. They make heroin out of them, don't they?

3   Purple toadflax is a summer flower with a silly name that often grows on old airfields and at the foot of walls. It's one of those flowers my grandma would savagely tear out, cursing: 'Filthy

weed!' But I like its lack of conformity and devil-may-care attitude. An anarchist's flower.

4   The primrose is often called spring's herald but unlike the poppy
and purple toadflax it's becoming harder to find. A delicate
yellow-petalled flower with a lettuce-leaf type leaf.

5   Flowering between May and December, the oxeye daisy is a great
meadow flower. It grows vigorously and looks magnificent in a
vase on the kitchen table, owing to its large wild flower heads and
toothy leaves.

6   If you can't identify the meadow buttercup without help, there's
no hope for you in the world of botanical taxonomy. What's to
say? It's yellow with sort of waxy-shiny leaves.

7   Lords and ladies are a very distinctive shade-loving plant flowering in April and May. The green berries that grow on the stem
after flowering turn bright red.

8   Characteristic purple scribbles and spots adorn the pink/white
flower petals of the common spotted orchid. Another summer
flower, this one, and one that often answers back, so don't put up
with any nonsense.

9   The snowdrop is a bit like a white bluebell really. It's absolutely
unmistakable, with long skinny leaves. It's early flowering. That's
all.

10 The cornflower is a kind of knapweed and is now endangered in
the UK. It has bright blue spherical-looking flowers and narrow
grey-green leaves that grow up the stem. It flowers in the summer,
often on waste ground. I hope you manage to spot one.

11 The yellow iris is an iris that is yellow. They like to grow on the
banks of ponds and rivers. A very striking and beautiful flower.
Tall, elegant and somehow related to the flamingo, just as the
thrush is somehow related to the wasp, and the robin to the bee.
It flowers in the spring and throughout the summer.

12 The honeysuckle or woodbind is a snarly climbing shrub with
flowers that smell delicious, especially to moths. An undeniably
intellectual summer-flowering plant with interests in philosophy

12. Honeysuckle

5. Ox-eye daisy

2. Poppy

4. Primrose

3. Purple
toadflax

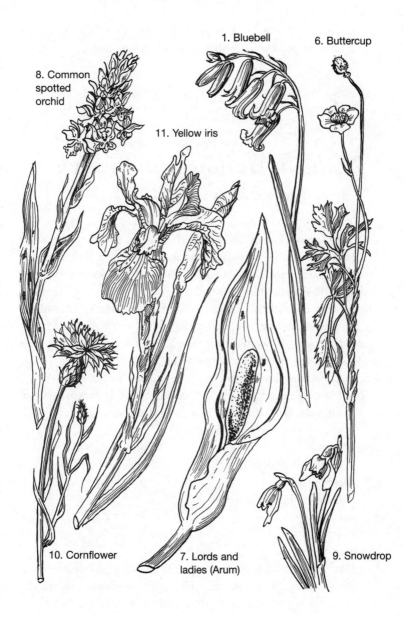

1. Bluebell

6. Buttercup

8. Common spotted orchid

11. Yellow iris

10. Cornflower

7. Lords and ladies (Arum)

9. Snowdrop

and music-theory. You'll often find it growing in hedges, though I had one on my fence that went all strange and ill-looking. I lopped its head off.

❀ *Poppy, Iris, Rose and Buttercup are popular girls names. Toadflax isn't.* ❀

How to
Make a Hallowe'en Pumpkin Jack-o'-Lantern

How delightful it is every 31 October – known also as Hallowe'en, All Hallows' Eve or Snap Apple Night – to find three spookily-dressed young rascals on the doorstep demanding money with menaces. 'Trick or treat!' seems to me a classic dilemma: a choice between two options, both disagreeable. This tradition may be the result of England having for years coupled Hallowe'en and Mischief Night (4 November), the time when youngsters played practical jokes on their neighbours: changing shop signs, whitewashing doors, and taking gates from their hinges. I suppose people didn't complain about boys removing their gates only because they didn't want them to take a fence. Sorry.

The Hallowe'en pumpkin jack-o'-lantern is the archetypal symbol of this autumnal festival. Here's how to go about making one.

REQUIRED
* *A decent-size pumpkin*
* *A marker pen*
* *A sharp knife (mind fingers)*
* *Some tea lights*

INSTRUCTIONS
1   Get yourself a decent-size pumpkin. This will probably have been grown in Spalding, the pumpkin capital of Britain, where the country's biggest producer grows about two million a year.

2   Draw a face on the skin.

3   Scalp the pumpkin so that you can get the seeds out. I favour a clean, circular cut; others prefer a zigzag.

4   Scoop out the seeds and membrane with your bare hands. This is a sloppy old process much beloved of nieces and nephews. Don't throw away the seeds. Instead, separate them from the 'string' (soul-destroying) and put them on a baking tray. Sprinkle with salt and bake slowly until crisp. They taste delicious, but take care not to burn them – I usually do.

5   Some 99% of pumpkins marketed domestically are used as Hallowe'en jack-o'-lanterns. Nonetheless, the flesh is edible and is yummy stewed and served with butter.

6   Carefully cut the features you have drawn. For friendly, use round and upwardly curved lines. For mean, use sharp and downward-pointing lines.

7   A charming 'spewing' pumpkin may be made by cutting the mouth in the shape of a large hole and pulling the seeds and stringy gloop out through the orifice. It's a delightfully suggestive arrangement, much admired by boys. (*See* fig. b.)

8   Put a couple of tea lights inside, wait for it to get dark and ignite the candles. You can put the top back on or not, depending on whether you do or don't like the smell of burnt pumpkin.

❀   *A serving of roast pumpkin seeds delivers about 285 calories.*   ❀

How to
Make a Macramé Bikini

Macramé is a kind of needleless, hookless textile-making process that requires no heavy machinery, depending as it does upon knots. In this respect it differs from both knitting and weaving. The main macramé knots are the square knot and the full and double half hitches. Hemp is the material of choice; the ropey bit, not the leaves, obviously, which are of no use at all and should be burnt.

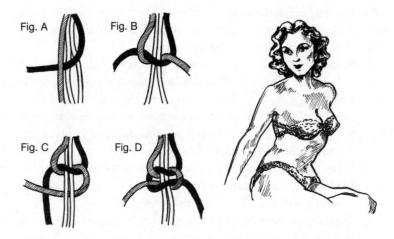

Fancy ornamental macramé was once favoured as a pastime by jolly bell-bottomed sailors, between their roistering, sextant-polishing and shanties. They used it to decorate their bits and bobs about the boat and would spend hours, bent intently over the hammock of Roger the cabin boy late at night, applying macramé embellishments to his auger crank before exhaustedly tossing themselves on to their bunks. Well, when your life consists of little more than rum, barnacles and concertina, you'll clutch at anything to invest your existence with a little gaiety.

It is recorded that seafarers would often compete to produce the most intricate macramé designs, and many cheery hours were occupied decorating their knife handles, bottles and wife-beating sticks. No, not wife-beating sticks, I made that up. They would supplement their income by selling their artefacts at ports around the globe, and would, if generous, occasionally give a native girl one for nothing. It was in this way that the art of macramé was introduced into many cultures across the world. Along with the pox.

GETTING KNOTTED
To begin, get yourself four suitable threads of string, twine or hemp cord. The general rule is to allow for a cord 10 times the length of your

finished article. The illustrations show the four filaments: one black, one shaded and, in the middle, two white. These two stay where they are as you make the knots. Those on the outside (shaded and black) do all the work.

HALF KNOT

1   Bring the (black) filament on the right over the two middle (white) strands.
2   Bring it under the (shaded) strand on the left.
3   Bring the (shaded) left hand strand under the two white filaments (Fig. A) and up through the loop made by the white thread and the black one (Fig. B). Is this making any sense?
4   Tighten the knot by pulling gently on the shaded and black threads.
5   Repeat this knot over and over to make a helix (spiral) (Fig. C).
6   Time for a glass of something.

SQUARE KNOT

1   Make a half knot as above.
2   Bring the shaded filament, now on the right, behind the two white threads.
3   Pass it over the black thread on the left.
4   Place the black thread into the loop on the right by going over the white filaments and under the shaded (Fig. D).
5   Tighten the knot by gently pulling the black and the shaded.

Now it's time to make your bikini so off you go. What do you mean, you thought I'd be giving you instructions? Look, it's taken up a page to describe two simple knots; you'll just have to use your initiative. Or do what others do and make a macramé bracelet. Easy!

❊ Itsy Bitsy Teenie Weenie Yellow Polka Dot Bikini *did well in Portuguese.* ❊

The World of Harps I
How to Play the Harp

When I played the cello in the school orchestra there were always three girls left packing their instruments long after the piccolos and violins had gone home: Andrea Wernish on the kettle drums, who I think became a tax lawyer; Olive St John on the doublebass (big nose) and Gail Vaughan Williams, who was alleged to be related to the late composer. Gail was both blonde and beautiful, and when she played she looked like an angel. Unfortunately her non-stop filthy swearing, spiteful bitchiness and plant-wilting BO endeared her to nobody. But she did look good on the harp.

Because of its beautiful mellow sound, the harp is the ideal instrument for beginners and it's one of the few instruments that men don't seem very interested in. Just running your thumb down the open strings makes a lovely sound, and even simple beginner's tunes such as *A B March* and *Three Blind Mice* sound good. This is in contrast to beginner's French horn or violin which will have the neighbours round with guns before you can say Bartók.

If you've tickled the ivories or played the organ then this is a good start to learning the harp. After all, the instrument is really just the insides of a piano turned sideways. If not, you are going to have to get used to reading two clefs at the same time and using both hands to make the notes. As a sort of signposting system all the F strings on a harp are black or blue and all the C strings are red or orange. That ought to stop you getting too far out of whack, though I don't remember ever seeing Marisa Robles staring at the strings and counting along.

INSTRUCTIONS
1   Cut your nails.
2   Position the harp between your knees and lean it back so that it rests on your right shoulder.

3　　If you look down at your feet, you may see some pedals (probably seven). If you do, you are using a big concert harp. These pedals are not accelerators and brakes as some beginners think; and neither do they do the same job as the pedals on a piano, sustaining or dampening the notes, they are there for changing the pitch.

4　　Start plucking. The only digit you don't use to play the harp is the little finger. You should know that the convention is that the thumb is numbered 1, index finger 2, middle is 3 and ring finger 4. You can vary the tonal quality by plucking with the fleshy part of your finger (warm and round tone) or the fingertip (brighter, louder), but not the nail.

5　　Try to look the part, like Gail Vaughan Williams, by closing your eyes and letting your elbows rise and fall. Sway gently backwards and forwards as you play, keeping your movements smooth and elegant with an ethereal smile playing over your lips, and allowing your wrists to wobble about a bit.

That's all there is to it.

Look, if you were expecting to be able to play the Krumpholtz sonata after reading a five-point guide, then I'm sorry to disappoint you. You can only really cover the basics in a book like this.

❈　*'Harpo' Marx's real name was Adolph.*　❈

The World of Harps II
How to Make an Aeolian Harp

The aeolian harp is one of those pesky things that is not what it says it is, like Welsh rabbit. Although it has strings, it isn't plucked, so it isn't a harp. It's played by the breeze blowing across the strings, often in a window, and is supposed to have been the instrument of Aeolus, the Greek god of draughts. The illustration shows how it might appear and if you'd like to make one – well, why not? – here's how.

REQUIRED

* *A shoe box with lid*
* *The flap from a corrugated cardboard box*
* *A pencil*
* *A ruler*
* *PVA glue*
* *A sharp craft knife*
* *Some elastic bands*

INSTRUCTIONS

1 Cut artistic 'f holes' into the lid with your craft knife and put it on the box.

2 Cut the flap of corrugated card into four ¾in-wide strips and trim them to the width of the shoebox. Glue these together in pairs, then stick them upright, one at each end, across the top of the box (*see* illustration). These are to form the bridges.

3 Stretch four or five elastic bands across the bridges. The bands should be tight, without deforming the box. Long skinny ones are best, and you can double the length of your strings by cutting and tying together shorter bands. Experiment a bit. It is better to have four strings of different tensions, but even a single-string harp will produce a sweet melody of notes that vary with the force of the wind.

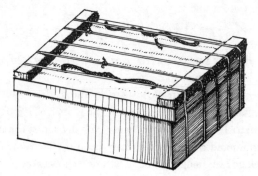

4   Place the box in the window. If it is a sash, lower it to create a small gap above the box, to focus the gale. You can stuff cushions in the side gaps for a similar reason.

Now listen. Usually what happens is that nothing happens, and you have to fiddle around for ages, adjusting window, box, elastic bands etc. This is called science. When it does work, however, it produces an ethereal music that sings to the deepest parts of one's amygdalae.

❁ *Winds in the northern hemisphere always blow clockwise.* ❁

How to
Press Flowers

Ronnie Barker once told me that he found the writing of an especially ingenious new lyric to a Gilbert and Sullivan song 'tricky but satisfying'. I remember his version of *Dear Little Buttercup* from *HMS Pinafore*, which finished: 'Dear little Buttercup / lift your left buttock up / you've squashed my opera hat flat.' I thought that homophone was so clever that I wondered why nobody had used it before. The artful rudery of Ronnie Barker – let alone the wit of the Savoy Operas – seems now to belong to an utterly bygone era, when gallantry was commonplace, when ladies still pressed flowers and swearing on television caused questions in parliament, when men were men and women were men dressed up.

So if you'd like to recreate that departed age and preserve a few of those smiling buttercups and the like with some old fashioned flower-pressing, here's the way to do it.

REQUIRED
* *2 heavy boards*
* *Several sheets of blotting paper*
* *A flower press (or car)*

213

INSTRUCTIONS

1   Get out there with your secateurs and bring back a selection of flowers while they're in the pink. Thistles, cacti and cauliflower don't press well but any delicate native bloom should work nicely.
2   Put a board on the table and then put five layers of blotting paper on top.
3   Carefully lay your flowers on the paper, spreading out the petals.
4   Put another five sheets of paper on top and another collection of specimens on top of that, sandwiching as many layers as you like.
5   Transfer to your flower press. If you have no press, you can improvise by laying another board on top and finishing with a few items of heavy masonry. Or better still, drive a car up on to the board. Be safe, obviously.
6   Leave for 30 hours or so and then carefully remove your specimens and put between fresh paper.
7   Press for a further 48 hours.

You can display your flowers on boards yourself or have them professionally mounted and glazed, over a verse in copperplate hand, such as Robert Herrik's: 'Gather ye rosebuds while ye may, / Old Time is still a-flying, / And this same flower that smiles to-day / To-morrow will be dying.'

What could be more charming?

❀ *Alan Titchmarsh's waxwork is one of Tussaud's 'most fondled'.* ❀

Skipping Games You Thought You'd Forgotten

S kipping games are as old as the hills. We used to spend hours at school jumping in and out of the whirling rope and I had a little puppy, his name was Tiny Tim; I put him in the bathtub to see if he could swim. He drank all the water; he ate a bar of soap – the next thing you know he had a bubble in his throat. In came the doctor; in came the nurse; in came the lady with the alligator purse. Sorry, I got completely caught up in a reverie there. How many girls even know what an alligator purse is these days, I wonder? Anyway, here is a guide to some of our finest skipping lore.

SOME SKIPPING TERMS EXPLAINED

* *Under the moon* or *front door*: running into a revolving rope that rises away from the skipper as it hits the ground.
* *Over the moon* or *back door*: running into a rope that rises towards the skipper.
* *Rope-rotation speed terms*: salt = slow; mustard = medium; vinegar = fast; pepper = very fast.
* *Keep the kettle boiling*: skippers line up to jump into the rope, which maintains a steady rhythm. The rope should never be 'empty'.

RUN-AROUND (REQUIRES AT LEAST FIVE SKIPPERS)

The skippers split into two groups, forming a queue on either side of the spinning rope. They now run in through the 'front door', jumping once and leaving from the same side. They then run round the rope-turner, go to the end of the queue on the other side and repeat the business.

FIVE, FOUR, THREE, TWO, ONE

An elimination game that gets harder as players drop out. On the first round each skipper enters the front door and leaves by the back door, running around the rope-turner back to her place while everyone shouts: 'Five, four, three, two, one.' Skippers must jump as indicated. A hesitation or a miss means expulsion. All skippers have a go before a second round is begun. Here's how it goes. The italics represent the *jump*.

> First round: *Five*, four, *three*, two, *one*.
> Second round: *Four*, three, *two*, one.
> Third round: *Three*, two, *one*.

Fourth round: *Two*, one.
Fifth round: *One* and *one* and *one*, etc

I LIKE COFFEE, I LIKE TEA
I like coffee, I like tea,
I like Matilda [more likely Chantelle or Fatima, these days] in
with me.

The nominee joins the skipper so that two are now skipping.

One, two, three, *change places*, seven, eight, nine, *change places*, etc.

On the command 'change places' the two change places until someone
messes up. Keep score as you go along.

I'M A LITTLE BUMPER CAR
I'm a little bumper car, number 48.
I went round the cooooooooooorner,

Here the skipper jumps out, runs round the rope and rope-turners, and
then jumps back in while the chanters maintain their cry of,
'cooooooooooorner'.

And slammed on my brakes.
A policeman caught me,
And put me in jail.
How many bottles of ginger ale?
Ten, twenty, thirty etc.

The rope is turned faster and faster until the skipper messes up or the
whistle goes and you troop in for maths. And, no, I don't know what
the ginger ale business is all about either.

❀ *10 minutes' skipping is as good for you as a 45-minute run. I'm told.* ❀

Understanding the zodiac

The term 'zodiac' is allegedly from the Greek meaning 'circle of little animals'. Zodiac signs are an infallible guide to one's disposition and likely future, but I don't believe in them because I'm Libra and Librans are very sceptical. The signs are set out below with their various attributes and characteristics.

Aries (the ram) March 21–April 20: born leaders who are easily irritated. You should avoid Virgos and Scorpios. Your lucky stone is sapphire; your lucky cereal is Special K; your lucky disease is necrotizing fasciitis.

Taurus (the bull) April 21–May 20: patient and reliable but can be greedy. Steer clear of Librans. Your lucky stone is gravel; your lucky sandwich is 'All-day Breakfast'; your lucky jargon is 'blue-sky thinking'.

Gemini (the twins) May 21–June 20: lively but sometimes superficial. Your lucky stone is kidney; your lucky shop is Marks & Spencer; your lucky disease is Hansen's (leprosy).

Cancer (the crab) June 21–July 20: sympathetic but can be moody. You should avoid Aquarians. Your lucky sandwich is sun-dried tomatoes and halloumi; your lucky jargon is 'going forward'; your lucky aeroplane seat is 26F (next to toilet *and* emergency exit).

Leo (the fish, sorry, lion) July 21–August 21: generous and creative but you always think you know best. Your lucky cheese is Wensleydale; your lucky disease is Sydenham's chorea; your lucky shop is Millets.

Virgo (the virgin) August 22–September 22: a reliable, shy worrier, prone to hypochondria (you sound a right bundle of laughs, girl). Your lucky song is *Chirpy Chirpy Cheep Cheep*; your lucky philosophy is Logical Positivism; your lucky sandwich is prawn and mayonnaise.

Librium (the neurotic) Septober 32–Octember 91: bold and confident. Avoid others. Your lucky cereal is All Bran; your lucky jargon is

Aquarius

Pisces

Aries

Taurus

Gemini

Cancer

Leo

Virgo

Libra

Scorpio

Sagittarius

Capricorn

'stakeholder engagement'; your lucky particle accelerator is CERN.

Libra (the scales) September 23–October 22: you don't like to rock the boat and can be a bit flirty. Avoid Taureans at all costs. Your lucky artist is Eric Ravilious; your lucky song is *Shaddup Your Face* by Joe Dolce; your lucky school subject is Citizenship.

Scorpio (the scorpion) October 23–November 22: exciting and passionate but can become obsessed. Your lucky disease is neurofibromatosis: your lucky shop is HMV; your lucky cleaning product is Toilet Duck.

Sagittarius (the archer) November 23–December 20: optimistic and jolly but prone to social faux pas. Avoid Cancer. Your lucky composer is Michael Tippett; your lucky alternative medicine is urine therapy; your lucky novel is *À la Recherche du Temps Perdu*.

Capricorn (the sea goat) December 21–January 19: ambitious and funny but a dreadful Scrooge. Avoid Gemini and Leo. Your lucky knickers are French; your lucky sandwich is cheese and ham toastie; your lucky astronaut is Buzz Aldrin.

Aquarius (the water bearer) January 20–February 18: friendly but you never know what you will do next. Your lucky number is 4,226.6; your lucky wrongly hanged man is Timothy Evans; your lucky hand cream is E45.

Pisces (the fish) February 20–March 20: kind and sensitive but easily fooled. Your lucky road sign is 'Pedestrians in the Road'; your lucky newsreader is Jon Snow; your lucky tinned food is Captain Holland's Cornish Scallop Soup.

❊ *The calendar we use was decreed by Pope Gregory XIII in 1582.* ❊

VII

How to be Bad

*All you need to know to be
a very naughty girl*

I am Catwoman. Hear me roar.

CATWOMAN

Belly Dancing for the Complete Novice

There's a mystical allure to belly dancing that you just don't get with clog or pole dancing, and the whole thing is steeped in history. There are even a few Persian miniatures dating back to the twelfth century depicting Middle Eastern terpsichore of this kind. The basic steps consist of a series of sensuous circular motions of one part of the body or another, such as the characteristic slow 'hula hoop' action of the hips and the cheeky pelvic tilt. The side-to-side 'Hindu head' and back-and-forward 'chicken head' are distinctive too, along with hip snaps, shimmies and a move that sounds like a pub: the 'Turkish arms'. For the more adept there is the balancing of baskets and swords, not forgetting the rich variety of unusual demonstrations with the exposed belly button. Let's be honest though, I don't have space here to turn you into a Mata Hari overnight, but with a few rudiments under your belt you should be able to give a good account of yourself on the kitchen tiles or bedroom carpet.

COSTUME

First you must dress the part. You'll need two or three yards of chiffon or silk or something, for your veil. Ethnic bangles are a must and you'll need to get hold of one of those tiny hats like a sequined bun to put on top of your head. A gorgeous, metallic pearly bra-thing with dangling coins will give you that desirable full-headlamp effect and a skimpy pair of bejewelled trousers, slit to expose the full leg and in a slinky material is de rigeur. I tried using a pair of my brother's 'banana hammock' speedos covered in glitter, with a bit of old net curtain tucked in, but it left something to be desired allure-wise.

You'll also need two sets of zils, those tiny finger cymbals, attached to the thumb and middle finger of each hand with a bit of elastic. Much of this stuff can be got at specialist suppliers, or you can improvise, depending on your level of ambition and what's in your wardrobe and on your dressing table. Long hair is better than short if you want to look authentic, as is a great deal of very black eyeliner.

A WORD ON NIPPLE TASSELS

Strictly speaking nipple tassels have no place in traditional belly dancing but with the rise in popularity of so-called 'exotic dancing' they can, I believe, be legitimately regarded as a related accoutrement. Nipple tassels come in two parts: the little conical caps, more properly referred to as 'pasties' (pronounced as in paste, not like the Cornish eatables), and the tassels themselves, thus allowing impoverished burlesque dancers the economy of just a single pair of tassels for attachment to a variety of pasties.

Attaching the pasties is as much art as science and the preferred adhesive is theatrical spirit gum. This is the stuff that actors stick their fake moustaches on with, providing a firm hold and being kind to flesh. My own experiments with Cowgum and gaffer tape resulted, it is true, in reliable adhesion but sounded on removal something akin to half a yard of tearing calico and made my eyes water like anything.

Once you've got the little darlings on, you need to practise the twirling. There are two main techniques for this. The first is to put your hands behind your head and bob up and down. The tassels should soon start to spin and you'll notice that they both twirl into the centre. If you wish to get them rotating in the same direction, you must vary your technique by bending forwards with your hands on your knees. Now rub your palms up and down your thighs, alternately left and right, standing up slowly at the same time. I confess that there is a problem with both these techniques and that is that they are pretty lacking in glamour – particularly the first, which makes you look as if you're sprinting for a bus without the benefit of mammarial support. One alternative is to try raising your arms, left then right. You should then be able to provoke a good spin – in opposite directions – while retaining your poise.

SOME SIMPLE BELLY DANCING MOVES

* *Basic belly dance position*: stand with your abdomen held in and your chest high. Your head should be up. Extend your arms in front of your chest as if embracing a pillar box, keeping a gap of

a foot or so between your hands, and put out your left leg as if you were stepping forward. Support yourself mainly on your right leg, the knee of which should be slightly bent. The left hip (the one with your extended leg attached to it) is the hip with which you will be leading the wiggling.

* *Horizontal hip thrust* move your hips backwards and forwards while twisting at the waist. This is not an up-and-down movement; think washing machine on rinse rather than space hopper. Hold your legs and upper body relatively static while you push your left hip forwards and right hip back, then reverse the move: right hip forward, left hip back.

* *Pelvic tilt*: possibly the most seductive belly dance move. From the basic position, bring your left leg back parallel to the right and push your buttocks forwards and upwards such that the base of your pelvis is lifted in the direction of the arrow (Fig. A). Reverse the move, causing your buttocks to stick out again (Fig. B). Combine the slants with a bend of the knees in the following way. Do three slants in a row, lowering yourself a little more with each tilt by further bending the knees, then unbend. Repeat the move a few times. But for goodness' sake do it sensitively girls or you'll look less like Salomé than a lady of the night. You can vary

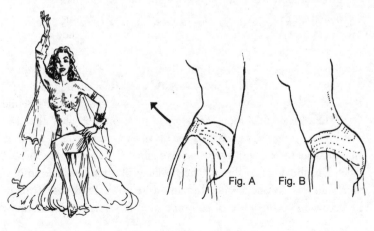

Fig. A   Fig. B

the speed of this move according to the musical pulse. Do not be put off by the 9/8 time signature, just count it like this: 1,2/3,4/5,6/7,8,9 and so on. In the mystic Orient, mothers rock their babies to beats like this.

* *Shoulder thrust*: a very easy but slinky move. Push your left shoulder forwards and the right backwards then reverse. Try to avoid giving an impression of Les Dawson in drag, making himself comfy. Slow and luscious is the thing to aim for.

* *Belly roll*: a great abdominal exercise, this one. First push your belly out – not too far or you'll look like Buddha. Then pull your belly in and hold this position as you lift your chest. Drop the ribcage and push your belly out again. It's in and out, a bit like the hokey-cokey but without shaking it all about. If you can manage a belly flutter (a vibration of the diaphragm), then go for it.

* *Veil removal*: what you basically do in this move is swoop your arms alternately in a large figure of eight, pulling the veil free as you do so. It's a bit like patting your head and rubbing your tummy, I'm afraid, so if it all goes wrong don't be disheartened. If you *do* get the hang of it you can combine it with any of the moves above.

Nothing could be simpler.

❀ *The 1st International Belly Dance Congress was at Bognor Regis in 2007.* ❀

How to
Charm a Snake

When I was small there was a programme on the telly called *The Herbs*. It was written by Michael Bond and featured a handful of animated characters with herby names such as Lady Rosemary and Sir Basil, Dill the dog and Bayleaf the gardener. But my favourite among them all was an enchanting Indian snake charmer called Pashana Bedhi, who slept on a bed of nails and used to sing a song containing the reassuring lyrics: 'Snakes that by me have been charmed, will not anyone be harming.' Nowadays this back-to-front syntax would doubtless be thought deeply patronising or even racist, along with Pashana Bedhi's huge 'stereotypical' turban, 'magic whistle pipe' and all-purpose Welsh/Indian accent. But I thought it was all lovely, and still do. Better than *Grange Hill*, anyway.

Like the making of top-notch children's television programmes, snake charming has been on the wane for quite a while, partly because it isn't easy to own a cobra in India (*or here*) and partly because of animal rights campaigners who say it is cruel. But if you've ever wanted to try it, here's how.

First get yourself a cobra. There are about 16 species and they are all venomous, though some more so than others. Get hold of a less venomous one (ask the man in the shop). This is the place for the health warning: snakebites are always nasty and can also occasionally be deadly. So practise with you on one side of a huge glass window and the snake (and a professional snake wrangler) on the other. If *he* gets bitten that's his problem.

REQUIRED (in addition to the snake, obviously)
* *A basket with a lid (like you've seen in the documentaries)*
* *A pungi (a flute-like instrument made from a* gourd*)*

DRESS
The traditional dress is a white turban, with a sprinkling of earrings and a shell necklace, plus a loin cloth and bare chest. But in your case – being a lady of the female persuasion – a lurex bathing costume is probably the thing to go for.

INSTRUCTIONS
1   Get dressed up, put your snake in his basket and sling it from a bamboo pole over your shoulder.
2   Now set up your stuff near Tesco, or somewhere you can get a crowd, and sit down cross-legged with the basket in front of you.

3 Remove the lid and begin playing your pungi. Your snake will slowly emerge and may extend its hood. This will happen without much effort from you because if you put any cobra in a basket for a while and then take off the lid it will naturally rear up as if roused from a snooze in a gentlemen's club. Standing is its natural defensive posture, along with the spreading of the hood, which will make it look bigger and more threatening.

4 Continue playing and sway to and fro; the snake will do the same, apparently hypnotized by the the music. In fact, snakes don't hear in the way we do, although they are sensitive to vibration. They are also alert to movement and will follow the swaying of your pungi.

5 Cobras are defensive by nature so it will take quite a bit of provocation to get your snake to bite you (not that you want him to). They prefer to rear up without striking and will do so in the wild for a long time, even when cornered. In addition, the pungi is a hard little instrument, and once it has been bitten a few times, it teaches your snake a useful lesson about the nature of fangs versus hard old gourd. In any case, you should sit out of striking range, which is only about $1/3$ of the cobra's body length. Obvious really. Once you get into your stride, you can, if you like, even kiss your snake on the head from above. Unlike some other snakes, cobras tend to strike downwards and can't bite anything above them. Anyway, once you know your snake, you can tell when he's had enough and is getting ready to bite you.

6 To persuade your snake to return to his container just stop waving your pungi and he will sink back into the safety and comfort of his cool basket.

I don't know why more people don't do it.

❀ *Originally, turbans were worn wet to cool the head in the desert heat.* ❀

Complete Whipcraft

We all remember Doris Day, don't we, in her wonderful Calamity Jane outfit, all boots and cap and tassels, belting out that song that went: 'Oh! The Deadwood Stage is a-headin' on over the hills, where the Injun arrows are thicker than porcupine quills.' Politically incorrect though the entire scenario is now thought to be, you can't but admire Doris's whip-cracking technique. And the men seemed to like it too.

There's no mystery to it. If you can beat a carpet, you can crack a whip, and there's no reason why you shouldn't have mastered circus- or Gypsy-style (vertical) whip-cracking within minutes.

EQUIPMENT

Whips go from about 4ft to 25ft and the best are stitched from kangaroo hide. They are made of four pieces in three sections: the handle, the 'popper' (the frayed tip that makes the noise), and the two leather pieces that comprise the main body, the 'thong' and the 'fall'. It is important to have a good whip. A cheap or lightweight whip lacks the proper weight to allow the vital loop to form (*see* below).

REQUIRED

* *The whip (try a 10–12ft whip, available from a number of British online shops)*
* *Sunglasses (cool) or goggles (uncool) to protect your eyes*
* *Gloves*
* *Jeans and a long-sleeved shirt*

HOW TO CRACK A WHIP

These instructions assume you are right handed. Just reverse them if you're not. The forward Gypsy-style crack is the whip-crack of choice, being pretty safe, very loud and fairly accurate.

1   Hold the handle in your right hand with the whip trailing *straight* out behind you, otherwise it will catch your leg as you bring it forwards. Your right arm should be hanging at your side, thumb pointing at the ground.

2   *The upswing*: quickly swing your arm forwards in a fluid upward movement so that your hand finishes above your shoulder, elbow completely bent, pointing at the target (say a tin can on a fence post), and your palm beside your right ear (Fig. A). The whip should be fully extended throughout the upswing and this depends on speed. While you are practising the upswing, allow the whip to fall behind you, without following through. Smooth please – no jerking.

3   *The follow-through*: as the popper starts to drop behind you, step forwards with the left leg and throw the whip forwards at the same time. Keep the thumb in position (palm towards ear) and snap the wrist as if casting a fishing line. You aim by pointing your thumb at the target and following through to that point. (You'll need a target to develop your technique properly.) As you throw the whip, its body will pass your shoulder creating a characteristic loop (*see point 4* below). Most beginners continue the

Fig. A   Fig. B

follow-through too far, throwing the whip so that it hits the ground. To avoid this, aim to finish the cast with your hand and arm pointing at the target. Don't snap the whip backwards. That's not what makes it pop.

4   *The loop*: The loop is essential. No loop, no snap. When you swing the whip up and position your wrist by your ear the popper is starting to swing down and forwards below your elbow. Now, when you cast the whip the tip will continue forwards past your body to make the loop (*see* Fig. B).

SAFETY

The popper can be going at about 700mph when you're throwing and you'll probably flay your legs occasionally, but covering up a bit will prevent you hurting yourself. It can also can pick up gravel and fling it around. Don't aim at people. In fact keep well away while you practise outside. Be very careful where you swing too. A whip can reach further than you think (especially behind you).

Indoors a long whip is probably a bit much. Maybe a short riding crop would be better, together with a leather cap, long black boots and a lycra cat-suit. All depends what you're doing really.

❀ *Doris Day's real name: Doris Mary Ann von Kappelhoff.* ❀

How to
Look Glamorous in a Sidecar

*M*aybe you're too young to remember sidecars, which have gone the way of washboards and petticoats. A sidecar was a kind of rigid bullet-shaped bubble just large enough to contain a girlfriend, which was attached to the port (left) side of a motorbike, supported on the road-side at the back by its own little wheel. Travelling in a sidecar in wet weather, you could pull over your head a perambulator-type hood with a plastic window at the front and sort of steam yourself into oblivion as you hurtled down a lane, alley or twitten, towards some fun.

Nowadays a few remaining sidecars are still to be seen zooming about, transporting girlfriends wrapped in warm blankets. They are referred to as 'outfits' by the dedicated band of enthusiasts who drive them. Communication with the driver is at last possible via a microphone, which is an improvement on the old days when you had to wait till your boyfriend decided to stop before you could speak to him, no matter how desperate you were.

If you find yourself pressed into a sudden sidecar caper, you should wear close-fitting clothes: jeans and a tight windproof jacket are recommended. Trainers or something equally serviceable will be needed on your feet. You'll also require a motorbike helmet and maybe goggles too to stop your eyes streaming like geysers. If you have long hair, tie it back securely or you will emerge with a hairdo like a horizontal witch's broom. Also, the seat can be a bit uncomfortable after about 30 miles – a comfy cushion helps a bit.

Come to think of it, I don't think it *is* possible to look glamorous in a sidecar. No, all in all and on second thoughts, maybe it would be as much fun to put on some music, light some candles and sit down with a Sidecar cocktail instead. Here's how to make one.

INGREDIENTS
* *2oz brandy*
* *1oz lemon juice*
* *1oz Cointreau*

INSTRUCTIONS
1 Combine the ingredients in a mixing jug with plenty of ice.
2 Stir and strain into a glass with a sugar coated rim.
3 Drink.

Yes, that's a better idea.

❀ *The London Sidecar Club has been going since 1950.* ❀

How to
Pull Off a Man's Shirt in a Twinkling

One of the most barefaced swindles ever conceived, the Shirt Steal was a favourite of the finest music hall double-acts of yesteryear. It's one of the funniest bits of stage business you'll ever see and, unlike an escape from a straitjacket inside a padlocked mailbag, it's a parlour trick very suitable for a lady. Here is my own postmodernist version, appropriate for close-quarters and ideal for the office knees-up or family function.

THE EFFECT
Following some cheerful belly dancing (*see* page 223) or the singing of a sentimental song or two, you ask a distinguished looking gentleman if he will help you with a little experiment. As he comes forward to a smattering of polite applause you comment on his smart clothes and ask if you may borrow his tie. Unwilling to appear churlish, he says yes. You now loosen the tie and slide it off slowly and seductively. This should provoke an expectant murmur, which will be suddenly checked as you whip out a wicked-looking pair of garden shears or kitchen scissors.

Ignoring the look of frank alarm on your gentleman's features you announce in a loud but somewhat uncertain voice, 'The Cut And Restored Tie is a very difficult trick for a lady. And it often goes wrong.' At this point your assistant snatches back his tie and begins rolling it up. You look hurt and remark, 'Well that's OK, I'll use your shirt then,' and seizing his shirt by the collar you suddenly yank it off, right over his head, leaving him standing there bare-chested in just his jacket, with his hair all up on end.

PREPARATION
Your assistant, as your audience may have twigged by now, is really a stooge. The best subjects for this jape are middle-aged professional-

looking gentlemen. Uncles and other male relations can often be roped in, as can complete strangers if you flutter your eyelashes a bit. They seem to enjoy both the limelight and the subterfuge. Maybe some of them also enjoy having their clothes boldly torn off in public by a lady, but let's not go into that.

A little preparation is required, of course; so not too long before the performance the two of you need to slip away unseen to set things up. Once you are somewhere private, ask your confederate to remove his jacket, shirt and tie. Be clear in advance about why you are asking him to do this; you don't want things to develop in untoward ways. On the other hand, if he's all gorgeous, there's no point in cutting off your nose to spite your face...

Anyway, back to business. Drape the shirt over his shoulders and do up the second and third buttons at the front. Dangle the sleeves down his arms and ask him to grasp the cuffs securely while he puts on the jacket. Once it's on, arrange the cuffs around his wrists but leave them unbuttoned. Draw the lower part of the shirt around behind him, tucking it under the back of his jacket, which you button up in front.

Next ask your accomplice to put on and tighten his tie but leave the top button undone. Now poke the tie neatly under the front of the jacket and, so long as he doesn't move about too much, things should appear quite normal. It is unfair to leave a man like this for anything longer than a few minutes so don't wait an age before you begin the performance.

PERFORMANCE
Follow the instructions set out above and when it comes to the point where you finally pull off the shirt, turn your assistant to face you with his arms relaxed at his side. Quickly undo the second and third buttons of his shirt and firmly grasp the back of the collar with both hands. In one swift movement, pull the shirt over his head and off. He will have to bend forward and hold still as you do this. The sleeves of the shirt often resist but a steady and firm tug does the trick. Try to make it smooth though – clinging on for dear life as your assistant writhes about with you in a humiliating tug-of-war spoils the effect.

As the shirt comes off, you will hear a roar of approval from your spectators, along with a few whistles if your assistant has a whistle-worthy chest. Before the hooting subsides, shake your man's hand and return his shirt. If your audience has realized that he is a confederate it will only add to their enjoyment, so make the most of it. Ask for a round of applause for such a good sport and take a moment to bathe in the reflected glory.

❋ *Detachable shirt collars were invented in 1827 in Troy, New York.* ❋

How to
Shave a Man

S hould you decide you are going to shave a man, you'd better take a close look at him first. You'll have noticed, I'm sure, that facial hair sprouts differently on different men. Some have a vigorous moustache capacity but little beard potential, others can grow sideburns like door-mats but have only the slightest of slight moustache latency, while a few are as hirsute as bears, with dense underbrush springing hourly from shoulders, chest, ears, legs, abdomen – *everywhere*. For these fellows, a lawnmower is the only answer, five o'clock shadow starting in earnest, as it does, at about a quarter-past-eleven. Often, though, their heads are excepted. It's a funny thing that otherwise hairy men are frequently as bald as ping-pong balls.

The point is that you don't need to spend ages shaving the chops of a man with only a faint chin whiskerage. Concentrate your efforts instead where they are most required. These instructions are, by the way, for shaving a man's *face* only.

INSTRUCTIONS

1 For a start, don't bother with low lighting, aromatic oils, candles and relaxing music. This is a *man*, remember. In my experience, they prefer a hard chair facing the sports channel, with the lights turned up bright enough for them to see their beer properly.

Naturally you'll need to put a pillow or rolled towel or something under his neck. You want him leaning back at a slight angle for best results. Try to get him to close his eyes – good luck.

2 Wash his face thoroughly with ordinary soap. As well as cleaning off the motorbike grease, this will start to soften the bristles.

3 Preparation is the key to success. You need that beard as soft as you can get it and you will be using exactly the same technique that you use when you do your legs. The only difference here is that some of the hairs you will encounter have the diameter of small saplings, so more shaving soap and time are required.

4 Fill a large bowl with hot water and soak a flannel in it. Wring it out and drape it over the chin and beardy part of your man's face. Hold it in place for about half a minute, pressing it firmly against his skin every now and then. You can repeat this step if necessary.

5 Now comes the shaving cream. You can use an old-fashioned shaving stick and apply the soap with a brush, or make life easy and squirt it from a can. I recommend the can approach because the brush technique is a skill in itself. Squirt a blob of shaving cream on to your palm. Not too much, you can always add a bit more, and smooth it evenly over the man's face and the bristly bit of his throat using a circular motion. You can spend a bit of time doing this. He will probably quite like it.

6 Use a new razor of good quality. Choose a famous name, not one of those little plastic ones that cost 99p for 100. Rinse it before you begin and again after each stroke. This will help you to keep the blades unclogged by bristles and will give your guy the closest and most comfortable shave. Don't shave him with your little pink ladies' razor – it's humiliating for a chap.

7 There are different places where you can start the shave, but a good one is from the 'top' of the beard, running in a vertical band down to the jaw line. Make a series of smooth, straight strokes, including the sideburn area. Light but firm. Generally, shaving with the grain is most comfortable, but you can get closer by

going against the grain. Doing it this way, though, can cause irritation of the skin (razor burn) so be as gentle as you can.

8   For any little nicks that occur (well nobody's perfect), a styptic pencil is the answer, not a torn out bit of the *Sun*.

9   To shave the neck and under the chin, I suggest that you go from the bottom of the neck upwards, which is against the grain. You just won't get a close enough shave in this area if you go the other way. You can make life easier by pulling the skin tight with the first and second fingers of your left hand, at the root of the neck.

10   To shave the moustache area, pull the upper lip down, holding it against the man's upper teeth, and shave downwards.

11   Finally, wash the fellow's face with very warm water, and gently feel for bits you might have neglected. Under the nose and chin are favourite spots for missing. Shave these areas and check with your subject for any areas he thinks could do with more attention.

12   When you've finished the shave, pad his face dry and apply a mild moisturiser. Men often go for the astringent burn of alcohol-based aftershaves but these can redden the skin.

13   A warm towel held over the face will ease any stinging.

Now dress your man in a nice dinner jacket and he can take you out to dine looking all lovely.

❀ *The red and white on a barber's pole represent blood and bandages.* ❀

How to
Strangle a Man With Your Bare Thighs

*H*ow often have you lain supine with a man standing over you making unreasonable demands? Most nights for some of us. When I first typed out the heading to this one I realised I'd put: 'How to strangle a man with your bare things.' I suppose that might be possible but it's not what I am going to show you. What I *am* going to show you is a good way to use a gentleman's weight against him so you can squeeze him into submission a bit like one of those snakes: cobra, no anaconda. You will be on your back with your legs bent and knees raised, feet flat on the floor. Your opponent will be standing over you. The pictures should help you get the idea.

INSTRUCTIONS

1 *The resolution*: take a deep breath.
2 *The grab*: with your right hand, clutch hold of his shirt second button down, or his jacket. If he is bare-chested and hairy grab a handful of mane, otherwise skin. With your left hand, firmly clasp the outside of his right biceps. Dig your fingers in if needs be (Fig. A).
3 *The pull-down*: using his high centre of gravity, suddenly pull the man down towards you.
4 *The hip-lock*: press your left foot into the bend in his right hip (Fig. B).
5 *The kick in the undergrowth*: with your right foot give him an almighty kick in the groin. This should curb his enthusiasm fairly smartly. He will probably say something along the lines of: 'Golly!' or: 'Oh, glory!'
6 *The head-positioning*: after the kick, bring your right leg straight out and over his left shoulder so that it is flanked by his left ear on one side, and your right arm on the other.
7 *The kick-and-pull-down*: kick/push his right hip with your left foot, which is already in position. At the same time pull him further down so that the left side of his neck is lying against the inside of your right thigh. His left shoulder is out of action now, held by your right thigh. Do not allow him to lie on your left leg: you need it for the next move.
8 *The armpit pin*: pull his right shoulder down so that his right armpit is pinned against the inside of your left thigh (Fig. C).
9 *The leg-lock*: bend your right knee, bringing your calf down over his left shoulder to lie perpendicular to his neck. Lift your left leg

and, bending it at the knee (where else?), put your right ankle inside the knee and tightly interlock your two legs.

10 *The right-arm hold-down*: press your left upper arm down on to his right wrist and forearm so that your left biceps and armpit hold it immobile. He will now be unable to pull your hair or poke you in the eye (Fig. D).

11 *The squeeze*: squeeze your hips and thighs together (you may have done this many times before, only in different circumstances) so that you cut off vital supplies of oxygen to his head. Test for unconsciousness by flicking his nose. If he jumps, he's just pretending. Once you are sure he is unconscious, get up and leave, or call the police. Or both.

The whole business happens in a moment, before he has time to gather his wits. But you'd better practise a bit first on a friend.

❂ *Meralgia paresthetica is burning pain in the thigh.* ❂

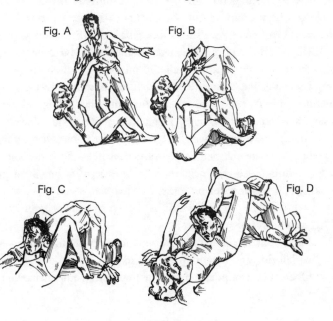

Fig. A   Fig. B

Fig. C   Fig. D

Wolf Whistling for Ladies

*T*here was a mistress at my school called Miss Dexter. She was known to us all, naturally enough, as Sinister Dexter, which we thought frightfully clever. But actually this was unfair as well as inaccurate, because Miss Dexter was the antithesis of sinister, resembling, as she did, Dame Margaret Rutherford in the role of Miss Whitchurch in *The Happiest Days of Your Life* (1950). Anyway, the thing was that she could whistle like a navvy and was able to call us in from the school boundary with an earsplitting shriek that would have given the Flying Scotsman a run for its money.

Of course, we girls used to practise like anything to get a good whistle going like Miss Dexter's, and there were two main schools of thought when it came to technique: the finger-whistlers and the non-finger. I belonged to the finger-sorority but I confess that neither group was much good, able to produce only a sort of osculatory sucking-wheeze, reminiscent of the sounds made by the black ooze of the great Grimpen Mire as it swallowed another horse.

Well, the other day, my American sister-in-law Marianne was round for lunch with my Auntie Sarah and me, and we discovered that *she* could whistle like a factory at five. What is more, after just a few minutes, my Auntie Sarah found that she was able to do it too. Though I struggled for ages, I failed, letting the side down badly. Nonetheless, in case you want to have a go, in a blow (literally) for sex equality, here are the definitive instructions, based on my sister-in-law's technique, so that next time you're passing a bunch of good-looking builders you can get in first.

THE MECHANICS
1   Hold your fingers in the position shown: thumb resting on the curled ring and fourth fingers of each hand.
2   Open your mouth and touch the tips of your fingers to the tip of your tongue.

3   Push your tongue back into your mouth like an accordion. You have now created a narrow channel inside your mouth and a small exit hole. By blowing forcefully through the gap – though not as hard as you think you must – you should start to hear occasional whistly sounds. Don't overdo it – it's easy to become light-headed.

4   Practise is the key to success so do not be put off by failure; keep at it while you are in the bath, watching telly, in bed and so on. After a while it will suddenly happen and you'll be whistling like an old pro. Don't try to learn it in church, though, because the noise – when it finally comes – is absolutely deafening and you'll simply blast the congregation off their pews.

5   As you gradually refine your technique, you'll discover that you can do the good-old *wheep-wheeoow* wolf-whistle as well as the *wheeoow-wheep* that Miss Dexter used so as to call us in from the south hedge, all those years ago. Whatever happened to her I wonder?

❀ *The wolf shares a common ancestry with the domestic dog.* ❀

How to
Write a 'Dear John' Letter

Oh gawd! How are you going to break off this romantic relationship compassionately? Sometimes the best way is an old fashioned goodbye letter, especially if the man is at a distance. So sit yourself down with pen, paper, wastepaper basket and a glass of water (not wine) and start your first draft. You'll do several versions, let me tell you. Here are some tips for avoiding a few of the beginner's mistakes.

1   Don't do it on the computer. Nobody wants to receive a printout, and it need hardly be said that an email or text message saying, 'You're dumped!' is simply not good enough from a lady. So use a pen, and be nice.

2   Don't start your letter 'Dear John…', unless you normally start that way. Begin with just his name, 'John…' and write in your usual style: not intimate in tone but friendly and kind.

3   Many men re-read their Dear John letters over and over. It helps the news sink in, so for goodness' sake be careful what you write.

4   Avoid blunt criticisms of his faults. Remarks such as, 'Your ears are not only hairy inside, but completely uneven and much too big,' or, 'You look like a sack of cauliflowers in bed,' may be true but are unnecessarily unkind. Spite is undignified; magnanimity should be the order of the day. And you do not want a thoughtless remark that you cannot un-speak to haunt you down the years. Certainly don't make unflattering comparisons such as, 'Aziz in Accounts really knows how to make a lady feel special,' or, 'Your legs look so spindly next to Gary's next door'.

5   Neither should you say things such as, 'You've stopped buying me flowers,' or, 'You used to be much more athletic,' because he might believe that a change in his behaviour can patch things up. It can't, or you wouldn't be writing a Dear John letter.

6   Be clear and unambiguous in your message. Tell him plainly that you are ending the relationship, and do this straight away. Don't leave it till after some news about how your grandma's hat was sat on by Mrs Winterbottom.

7   Admit that the decision has been a hard one for you to make (if it has), and that in writing you have had to marshal all your courage and resolve.

8   Say that the relationship has not been right for some time and tell him frankly that you are not right for each other. These are useful clichés that allow for fault on both sides, and they underline the

finality of your decision. He will doubtless recognise the truth in what you say, and see that you have made up your mind.

9　Let's be honest, you are probably not a saint yourself, and it might help to admit this to him. Don't though, whatever you do, pour out a long confession of your serial infidelity, containing lurid details of the magnificent threesomes in his flat with the lead guitarist and drummer of The Sex Pests while he was doing his voluntary work with the underprivileged. It will just cause him unnecessary pain.

10　Be exclusively positive about him and wish him well for the future. This lets him know that, although you don't want to continue the romantic relationship, you have not completely written him off as a human being, and that you still respect him and hold him in some regard as a man. You do, don't you?

11　It is best not to suggest staying friends or being 'just friends'. This seldom works and can be a torturous encumbrance for him. A clean amputation heals quicker.

12　Stay amiable in your sign-off. Use your first name. There's no need for 'Yours faithfully' but don't use the word 'love' either or put little kisses. You'll just undo all your hard work and confuse the hell out of him.

13　Once you've written your letter, *set it aside for a few days* to let the body heat go out of it. Before you send it, read it again critically to make sure you have said exactly what you mean. It can be a very difficult thing to do.

REPLIES

What if you receive a reply? Well, it's up to you now; I can't run your whole life for you. With any luck, he will have understood and you will be spared the experience of a friend of mine who wrote a Dear John letter to her soldier boyfriend and received in reply a parcel containing a photograph of herself along with a whole load of pictures of other girls – the sisters, girlfriends, and cousins of other members of his platoon, she guessed. A short note on the back of her original letter read: 'Dear Amy, I forget which one is you. Just take your picture out and send back the rest. Cheers, Adam.' At least he had a GSOH.

❀ *The quill pen was introduced around 700 CE.* ❀

How to
Do a Striptease

*T*hings have come a long way since the striptease was routinely described as 'tit for tat'. In December 2006 a Norwegian court ruled that it is in fact an art form and is therefore exempt from VAT.

It's an old one too, with Sumerian tablets depicting the descent of Inanna into the Underworld, removing an article of clothing at each of the seven gates, somewhat reminiscent of Salome's dance of the seven veils in the New Testament. Anyway, if you'd like to try this art form (and why not?) here are a few pointers.

INSTRUCTIONS

You don't need to be a supermodel to do a striptease; all you need – apart from the outfit – is confidence. Stockings and suspender belt are a must, and no big pants please girls – try a thong. During the strip keep eye contact with your man and use flirty body language: flick your hair, gyrate your hips and keep one leg in front of the other, heel lifted, whenever you can. This is a classic model's trick that can help to ameliorate the ungainliness of some awkward poses, making your legs look longer and leaner.

1   Start by putting on some music. Choose something sensible. *The Stripper* is trite, *Onward Christian Soldiers* is all wrong, and you'll just never keep up with *The Flight of the Bumble Bee*. Something moody with a strong pulse is what you need.

2   Now begin strutting up and down: chest out and head up. Picture a figure of eight and follow it with your hips. As you move, place one

foot directly in front of the other, tightrope style for maximum femininity, arching your back, with tummy in and boobs out. Confidence is the thing: you must show your man that you're in charge.

3   Use a scarf or feather boa as a plaything, representing... well, never mind. Draw it alluringly through your fingers and over your shoulders, or use it as a blindfold on your man. Drape it around his neck and pull him towards you. By the way: *he is not allowed to touch you* at any time.

4   The first item to come off should be your jacket. Do this slowly, looking backwards at him over your shoulder. Unbutton the jacket and slide it down and off in one movement. Rolling about on the floor desperately trying to wrestle your arms out is not right: you may be stripping but you're not teasing.

5   The skirt is next. Turn your back again, look over your shoulder and unzip your skirt. Do this slowly, not as if you are a coroner opening the third body bag of the day. Keep your bum sticking out and arch your back as before. Remove the skirt in one quick but smooth movement, letting it drop. Once it's on the floor, step out of it. Don't pick it up all neat and tidy; there's nothing less seductive than someone folding her pants or hanging something up on a hanger. And don't allow it to snag your feet. Staggering around all out of balance with ankles snarled up and then plunging to the carpet lacks panache.

6   Likewise, you can spoil the whole effect if you have to stop, bend down and undo your shoes. If you are wearing sexy strappy things leave them on. Otherwise wear something easily slip-offable. Just lift your leg behind you, reach down and remove the shoe as artistically as you can. I know Dr Martens are all the rage in the magazines girls but *not for a striptease please.*

7   Now for the stockings. Maintaining eye contact, put your leg up on a chair. You should be presenting a profile to your man. Undo the suspenders and sexily roll the stocking off with both hands, keeping your bum high. Once the stocking is over your heel, lift it away between finger and thumb. Repeat with leg 2.

8   Frankly, suspenders look a bit daft without stockings so unclip the thing with dispatch and poing it at him naughtily. Without taking his eye out if you can help it.

9   The bra is next. Try to make the most of this because he's probably been especially looking forward to this bit. Stand in front of him and wriggle out of the straps. Do it slowly, not like a market-dame. Turn away and look back over your shoulder. This over-the-shoulder look you keep using is primitive come-on body language that all men recognize. Undo the bra but hold it over your boobs with one hand. Turn back to face him looking foxy and keeping an arm across your breasts to hold the bra in place. Pull it out slowly from underneath with the other hand and let it fall. Keep your boobs covered for a moment, then draw your arm away, caressing your frontage as you go. Now make the most of things by weighing the evidence in front of you, and spend a bit of time 'tuning the radio channels'. This should keep him fairly interested.

10   Right, you are now down to your thong. I hope it's a thong – or something similar – and not a great big pair of flesh coloured elasticated support pants. You've got to take them off like a proper porn-star not like some Edwardian Grandma peeling off her

bloomers for the summer, so don't keep your legs together as you get 'em off, or it will look hideously wrong. Instead, use your model's trick of placing one leg in front of the other and lifting the heel elegantly. Now for the big finish: offer your man a profile view, put your hands inside the knicker elastic at each side, palms against your legs, and lift the band up and away from your body. Now slide your hands down your legs, bringing the panties along. Bend your body gracefully as your hands move down past your knees and let the garment drop to the floor. It's easy to finish on a bum note because stepping artistically out of a scrunched thong is a bit tricky. You can find it snarls around your foot in a most inelegant fashion. Sorry, you're on your own here: just take it slow.

11   Now promenade around your man caressing yourself, until he is overcome with emotion and something pops.

❀ *Gypsy Rose Lee (Rose Louise Hovick) starred at Minsky's Burlesque.* ❀

How to
Escape the Next Date

$\mathcal{T}$here are many reasons a relationship might go stale and I'm not going into them all here. The point is, though, that sometimes the next date suddenly seems about as desirable as watching a post mortem. So here are a few ideas that will allow you to slip your collar the next time you want to escape a date.

The creeping realization that things are bad often comes upon you while you are already on a date and this can be a good time to make your action plan live. I'm assuming that you really don't like him and never want to see him again, so there's no place here for mild evasions and excuses: you've got to go in for the kill. Use the freelancer's technique of never saying no to a job. Instead get him to turn *you* down. The way to do this is to make yourself completely un-dateable by being totally embarrassing or vile.

INSTRUCTIONS

* If you're already out on a date, blow your nose on the tablecloth.
* Drink too much and start shouting.
* Pinch every male bottom in sight (waiters are good).
* Order the most expensive dish on the menu with Champagne and then leave it.
* Develop a maniacal laugh and a strange twitch.
* Wink at the men and order them all drinks on his card.
* Demand that he choose there and then between you and his mother or between you and sport.
* Wear a knee-length tweed skirt and pop socks.
* Stop shaving your legs.
* Stop washing your hair.
* Smear on your makeup disgustingly.
* Become embarrassingly opinionated.
* Take up Churchillian cigars.
* Stop brushing your teeth.
* Wear a shell suit with a filthy slogan on it.
* Stop changing your clothes.
* Begin loud and very public burping.
* Ring his friends and arrange dates with them all.
* Never just stand him up. That would be unladylike.

❀ *Date palms take about seven years to bear fruit.* ❀

How to
Hide a File in a Perfect Victoria Sponge

Suppose your man has been fitted up by a grass and had his collar felt by the rozzers who then verballed him, saying he sang like a canary after 'falling down the stairs'. Now the beak has banged him up with a load of nonces and mean screws so it's up to you to spring him. Do you have a clue what I'm talking about? Because I don't. The old file-in-the-cake-trick is the way to go. This is what you must do… (Crossfade to long shot of prison. Exterior. Night.)

Ingredients

* *8oz caster sugar*
* *8oz butter (soft)*
* *8oz self-raising flour*
* *4 eggs, beaten*
* *1tsp baking powder*
* *2tbsps milk*

Filling

* *Whipped cream*
* *A jar of good raspberry jam*
* *Icing sugar (for the top)*
* *A small but sturdy file*

Instructions

1 Heat oven to 374° F / 190° C / Gas Mark 5.

2 Butter two 8in sandwich tins and line with greaseproof paper.

3 Beat ingredients (except for jam, cream and icing sugar) to a smooth consistency so that it drops off the spoon.

4 Dilute with water if too thick.

5 Divide the mixture between the tins and drop the file into one of them. Smooth off the surface and bake for about 20 minutes or until golden. The one with the file may cook slightly faster as the metal heats up inside. When done, the cake should spring back if you depress its surface.

6 Turn out the tins and cool on a rack. You will clearly see the file shape on the base of one of them, where it's sunk to the bottom. Turn this one flat-side down.

7 For the filling, spread the jam generously over the bottom sponge.

8 Spread cream over the other (the one with the file in it) and

carefully position on top. Dust with a little icing sugar. The Duchess of Royston would probably do this through a doily to make a pretty pattern.

Take the cake along to the prison on your next conjugal visit and cross your fingers.

❀ *The Victoria sponge is so called after the British monarch of that name.* ❀

How to
Seduce a Man

The thing you need to understand about men is that they are not like you when it comes to selecting a mate. For a woman, a man must pass a number of implicit tests before he will be considered suitable. Among the physical hoops he must jump through are height (tall better), masculinity (aggressiveness, strong jaw, large nose, strong forehead, wide shoulders, shorter index finger than third finger) and power (high-earning job, status-symbols: e.g. expensive car, house, watch and clothes).

But these good-mating or 'Tarzan' indices must be counterbalanced by good-fathering skills. So qualities such as humour, sensitivity, strategic thinking, playfulness, charm and being brainy will also count.

In contrast, a man just wants the prettiest girl he can find right now. Of the three famous qualities – brains, breeding and beauty – that a girl is supposed to require so as to get on, beauty heads the list; a beautiful checkout girl will be more desirable to a man than a plain princess. Being smart and polished will help, of course, as will serving up a delicious dinner, but those women who say the way to a man's heart is through his stomach are really aiming too high. The physical qualities a man responds to are not really to do with being thin, though. Tall is good, as is an hourglass figure, which transmits the message: *I can have babies and feed them*, but what really pulls men, beyond the first suck of Neanderthal attraction, is a positive temperament. Men greatly prefer enthusiastic, cheerful adventurous women, even if they do not look like Marilyn Monroe (*who does?*). Confidence is a huge aphrodisiac for a man, so if you are exciting and upbeat rather than negative, moany, critical and lugubrious you already have a huge advantage in the seduction stakes and an inbuilt capacity to outlast the gormless Barbie dolls, whose attraction withers for many men, once they open their mouths to speak.

SEDUCTION: A LIST
Here are a few things you can do to help along what is already not a difficult job. Think Mrs Robinson in *The Graduate*.

* Wear things that emphasize your best bits. Legs, boobs, neck, arms, abdomen. If you're lucky enough to be good all over, conceal some of it.
* Get close to him.
* Pay him proper attention. Listen attentively and look into his eyes. If his pupils are dilated, you know you are having an effect. Either that or you are down a mine.
* Look at his mouth while he speaks. Don't gape; move in a triangle between eyes and lips.
* Lean towards him while licking your lips. Be subtle about it; you don't want to look as if you've just eaten a bucket of the Colonel's fried chicken.
* Play with your hair.
* Stroke your thigh.
* Whisper a question to him.
* Touch him. Grab his watch to check the time; push him playfully when he says something amusing; accidentally bump your knee up against him; lean up against him, tuck a loose hair behind his ear.
* If sitting, cross and uncross your legs (men find this extremely alluring, especially if you have long legs and a short skirt).
* Ask him to blow on your neck. Any excuse will do.

* Ask him to help you undo your top shirt button or attach your necklace. Is he dribbling yet?
* Tell him you are cold and ask him to warm your hands.
* Men are very visual creatures. Tell him you are thinking about buying a swimming costume and ask him which type he thinks would best suit you.
* Dip your finger in your ice cream and offer it to him to taste. Are his cheeks flushing? If so, you're doing OK.
* Grasp his knee then slowly advance up his thigh squeezing as you go, but stop before you get to the shorts line.
* Talk about vaguely erotic – or frankly erotic – things. One of my friends always talks about her Brazilian wax to men she's interested in. Their tongues just fall out.
* Sit playfully on his lap (this is an absolute killer for chaps. Especially if you wriggle about a bit). You may well notice an effect. That's all I'm saying…
* If he asks you back to his place, make sure you don't end up like the James Thurber cartoon, where the man is saying to the lady: 'You wait here and I'll bring the etchings down.' Bad result.

❋ *In* The Graduate *Anne Bancroft was just six years older than Dustin Hoffman.* ❋

How to
Spot a Love Rat

Women, it has been alleged, use sex to get what they want whereas men are unable to do this because sex *is* what they want. It is one of those observations, like 'aspirins are small' and 'dusters are yellow', that seem obviously true.

The problem comes when your man is unable to confine his wants and starts spreading himself around in contravention of the 11th Commandment: 'Thou Shalt Not Cheat On Thy Bird.' It's a bit like the coveting your neighbour's wife one. If you are harbouring a suspicion that your man might be a rumpler of other girls' sheets, now's the time to rate your date.

Some men are more likely than others to cheat on their women, and a gentleman's personality profile and attitudes can reveal the likelihood that he will do the dirty on you. Have a go at the questionnaire below and see how you get on.

THE LOVE RAT CHEATER-PROFILE SCREEN

1 Does your man love action and thrills? Sky-diving and fast-car men look for thrills wherever they can get them. Be warned, their dangerous sports can include playing with fire and playing away.

2 Is he thrusting, powerful, charismatic and ambitious (JFK syndrome)? That charismatic thrusting will not stop this side of your bedroom door.

3 Did his dad cheat? Boys learn how to treat women from their dads.

4 Do his chums cheat on their girls? Birds of a feather flock together. As do blokes.

5 Does he have a vigorous bed-history? Don't expect him to confine his vigour just because he's met you. Simple as that.

6 Does he know lots of ladies? Contacts with female women of the opposite sex can turn into romps before you can say Norwich. The more girls he's friendly with, the greater the numerical risk.

7 Is he relaxed about the male infidelity thing and has he been unfaithful to previous girlfriends? Well then, why should he rein himself in now? Cheaters remain cheaters: and a cheater never changes his spots. If you answered yes to this one look out!

8 Does he often come home covered in blonde hairs and lipstick, with other girls' pants in his pocket? You may be entitled to the first faint flickerings of doubt.

The more yeses you got, the more likely you've landed a love rat. What you do with him now is entirely your own affair…

❋ *'NORWICH' stands for Nickers Off Ready When I Come Home.* ❋

How to
Turn Down a Rotten Marriage Proposal

One of the problems of being a young lady, of course, is boys and knowing how to handle them. It's something I think you learn on the job – if you'll pardon the unfortunate idiom. Like choosing cushions, rejection is one of those things that is largely the responsibility of the female, and it can take a while to learn how to do it with grace and charm.

Suppose some gentleman of whom you are fond, but no more, suddenly presents you with an engagement ring at dinner or goes down on one knee, what are you going to do? First of all, *never* say yes if you don't really mean it or you'll end up like Nancy Astor, who remarked: 'I married beneath me, all women do.'

Here is the proper way. I'm assuming that you are a *lady* and not some scabby toothless chav for whom a 'Naaaaah!' between fag puffs, will be sufficient. And unless it's one of those creepy 'stalker' types, text messages and emails are plainly unsuitable.

INSTRUCTIONS

1   Be honest but kind. Don't say: 'Harry, you are nice but I don't fancy you and would *never* marry you, because of your effeminate passive demeanour and those skinny chicken-legs, and your low-level job with Airfix, and your lack of a sense of humour, and your awful mother and your BO.' Instead make it crystal clear in polite terms that, though you like him, you *do not want to marry him.*

2   Don't apologize.

3   If he keeps up a protest about how you were made for each other, use the broken-record technique: repeat that though you like him you definitely don't want to marry him. If the message doesn't get through after repetition, you are flogging a dead horse. Go on to the following points.

4   If you find an engagement ring in your pudding at a restaurant, just swallow it.

5   Explain that marriage to anyone is not your cup of tea at the moment. Notice the clever use of words?

6   Ask your father to refuse permission for your hand (and the rest of you).

7   Claim lesbianism.

8   For the man who is still not receiving, hire a hoarding in Leicester Square with the bald message: 'Earth calling Harry Bloggs of Number 2 Neville Gardens. Get it into your fat head: Mavis Davis does not want to, and WILL NEVER, marry you!

❋ *Zsa Zsa Gábor has been married nine times.* ❋

How to
Ride a Space Hopper in a Miniskirt

The 1970s seemed like Limbo when we were in them, but now everybody looks back through rose-tinted non-National Health spectacles and says how wonderful it was to sit on a wall all day, bored rigid in purple flares – the *only* item of clothing ever to be refused by Oxfam on grounds of taste. Just count yourself lucky you're too young to remember them (if you are).

Amongst the stupid products available during the 70s was a device for flipping your LPs forwards one at a time so you could select one (made by K-Tel). This saved you having to use your finger. Then there was the legendary Brush-O-Matic, also made by K-Tel which – wait for it – brushed your clothes. All the boys rode bicycles called 'Choppers' which had dangerous looking gears situated between the seat and the handlebars, and all the girls bounced up and down on space hoppers, huge inflatable orange balloons with a silly face on.

Space hoppers were fun, if slightly unladylike. We even had some at school, which we were encouraged to ride by Miss Snellgrove during warm-ups in PE. Miss Snellgrove was a gym mistress of such obviously Sapphic tendencies that we presumed she was really just hoping for a flash of knicker elastic. She wore men's football boots I remember, had hair like Wilfrid Hyde-White, smoked a pipe and, though her first name was Monica, insisted on being called Bernard. *I'm not making this up.* Anyway, you can still find space hoppers here and there so here's the way to ride one in a miniskirt, based on the Snellgrove technique.

Snellgrove method

1   *Knicker-choice*: balance good looks with good coverage (just in case).
2   Straddle your hopper with feet on the ground in front to stabilize you, and the handle between your legs. Handles come in two forms: (A) twin horns and (B) a sort of spade handle. The latter will better conceal your knickers.
3   Give a couple of gentle bounces to get a feel of the spring potential.
4   Leap into the air keeping the hopper between your legs but instead of landing on your feet lift them up by bending your knees, landing instead on the space hopper's big round bum.
5   Place your feet back on the ground moments after you land and spring off for the next bounce.
6   Change direction by pushing off harder with your right foot (to turn left) and left to turn right.
7   *Always bounce with the wind behind you*. I've seen the skirts of careless girls simply blown inside out.

❋ *K-tel was founded in the 1960s in Winnipeg, Manitoba.* ❋

How to
Slide Down a Fireman's Pole

*T*hose music hall comics produced some long-lasting jokes – not good maybe, but durable. I was in The Cask And Glass the other day when I overheard the following: 'Is anything worn beneath the kilt? No, it's all in full working order.' That must have been old 100 years ago.

What is it about a man in a kilt? Or a marching band of pipers in kilts? It makes me go wobbly all over: all those buckles and knives and pipes and bright colours and huge great fuzzy hats. There's something about uniforms that provocatively emphasize the masculine characteristics of the wearer, which appeals. And you can take your pick, from soldiers and sailors, from pilots, policemen, from storm troopers and even from traffic wardens. Well, maybe not traffic wardens. But I reckon near the top of the list must be the fireman in uniform.

So I wondered, would it be possible to persuade a fireman to show me how to slide down his pole? I'd already read that the first firemen's poles were introduced in the time of horse-drawn fire engines, when firemen lived above the stables. I had also noted that a spokesman for West Midlands Fire Service boasts the longest pole in Europe – some 40ft of it. Good Lord Sir, that's a huge one!

The trouble is that firemen's poles have recently come under the health and safety microscope with reports of poles being omitted from a new West Country fire station because of the danger that firemen might suffer 'chafing to the thighs'. I would like to put it on record that I hereby volunteer to massage soothing ointments into the thighs of any fireman suffering intercrural distress. Just contact the publisher.

In the end I managed to speak to a very helpful senior fire officer and would like to record my thanks to Group Manager Clive Eustice of the London Fire Brigade for his help with this one. I would *like* to thank him but all he said was:

> *You wrap your legs round the pole at the ankles and that's about*
> *it, to be honest. Your hands are used only to balance but you can*
> *do it without them. The speed of decent is controlled by the legs*
> *although most poles aren't long enough to worry about that – just*
> *wrap and drop!*

So in light of the paucity of the information provided, and the news that members of the public aren't allowed to slide down firemen's poles, I am withholding my thanks. If you have better luck than me in trying to slide down a fireman's pole, I'd be pleased to hear your story.

❁ *A flame is a self-sustaining, oxidising chemical reaction producing energy.* ❁

How to
Swing Upside-Down on a Trapeze

When I was young I used to have a Ladybird book called *The Circus Comes to Town*. The pictures were so evocative that when the circus really did come to town I begged my parents to take me. The big top, the dashing ringmaster and hilarious clowns, the lions and tigers and gaudy elephants, the sawdust, the roar of the crowd – you know, all the stuff. Well we ended up at the Fairfield Halls in Croydon – a malodorous aircraft hangar of a place, where Charlie Cairoli the famous unfunny Franco-British clown was ending his career. There were no lions, no sawdust and no big top. I do however remember a troupe of trapeze artists in sparkling costumes, but I may have transplanted them into my memory from their exciting page in *The Circus Comes to Town*.

Anyway, in case you decide, after all, not to work in a call centre but to become a magnificent woman on the flying trapeze instead, here are the basics. *Please* use a safety net.

Hanging by your knees

1 Grab the bar with both hands and start swinging until you have a bit of momentum going.

2 When you're ready, pull up your knees between your chest and the bar. Slide your feet over the bar so that it finishes behind your bent knees. Bring your heels close to your thighs. Maintain a good swing as you do this, if you possibly can.

3 Keeping your knees tightly bent, let go with your hands, and uncurl your body as gracefully as possible, letting your arms fall towards the floor.

4 Keep swinging by alternately arching your back and throwing your arms forwards.

BEING CAUGHT BY A MAN

1   Facing away from each other, you must now swing towards each other very carefully. Timing is of the essence: you must meet at the highest point of your swings. Don't go too fast or you'll both crack your heads open.

2   As the person being caught, it is your responsibility to help the catcher. Arch your back with your head thrown back and your arms above you in a rigid pose like Superwoman.

3   With your head thrown all the way back, you'll see everything back-to-front and upside-down. Just as you are getting used to this crazy view you will become aware of a man in a leotard (your partner) hurtling towards you unstoppably, like a demolition ball on the end of a chain. As soon as you feel him grab your wrists, release your knees so that your trapeze is freed, swinging away 'empty'. You will now be dangling – and swinging – dramatically from the arms of your catcher, high above the crowd.

4   If he misses or drops you, try to land in a safety net rather than on a concrete floor, which can be somewhat unforgiving.

❀ *The French acrobat Jules Léotard invented the leotard.* ❀

Index

Numbers in *italics* refer to illustrations.